Praise for
Outlive Your Life

"*Outlive Your Life* is a road map for your life journey that will leave you few regrets and will inspire you to be all that God intended. This is one of those rare books that can change your life."

— Richard Stearns
President, World Vision US; and author, *The Hole in Our Gospel*

"Pastor Max tells all folks how to move from Bible studies to Bible doins."

— Denver Moore
Best-Selling author, *Same Kind of Different as Me*

"A powerful collection of stories and biblical truths that will keep you awake long after you read it, wondering and, hopefully, scheming how to outlive your life."

— Ron Hall
Best-Selling author, *Same Kind of Different as Me*

"Some books change the reader; some books change the world. This book will do both. This astounding writer has shaped my worldview for twenty-five years. With this book we all can enter into a practical partnership to expand the kingdom and care for the vulnerable."

— Dr. Joel C. Hunter
Senior pastor, Northland, A Church Distributed

"Master storyteller Max Lucado reminds us that the gospel must be good news for everyone in our world—and of the joy that comes with serving as Christ's hands and feet in a world that needs us."

— Jonathan T. M. Reckford
CEO, Habitat for Humanity International

"The only way of changing the world for good is for Christians to take seriously our call to be the light of Christ. My friend Max is calling the church, which is you and me, to be the church—to love and serve one another through Jesus Christ."

— Chuck Colson
Founder, Prison Fellowship and Colson Center for Christian Worldview

"This may well be the most important book you will read this year . . . or for several years. Max Lucado always writes with simple grace, beauty, and imagination. Here he opens his heart in a way that will—or should—break your own heart open, up, and out in ways that will bless you beyond your imagination."

— Leighton Ford
President, Leighton Ford Ministries

"This book is a call to arms—both yours and mine—to embrace those who have little or nothing. As Max Lucado says, 'the challenge can create a team.' Won't you join our team and invest your life in something that will live, nourish, and give relief long after you are gone? Read this book and see how you can make a difference right where you live."

— Luci Swindoll
Author and speaker, Women of Faith®

"Millions have received the gift of compassion from the writings of Max Lucado. Now he gives us another gift—the call *to* compassion. Read and unleash."

— John Ortberg
Pastor and author, Menlo Park Presbyterian Church

"Every now and then you hear a call that is so clear, so true, that you know without a shadow of a doubt it comes from the very heart of God. This book contains such a call. If we listen, it just might change the world."

— Sheila Walsh
Speaker, Women of Faith®; and best-selling author, *Beautiful Things Happen When a Woman Trusts God*

"What does it really mean to 'love thy neighbor'? Max Lucado suggests that our *neighbor* is not only the family next door but also the one struggling for survival on the other side of the globe. *Outlive Your Life* is an inspirational call for Christians to put their faith into action and reach out to those in desperate need."

— Jim Daly
President and CEO, Focus on the Family

"Max Lucado demonstrates what the compassion preached by Jesus in the Beatitudes looks like when it is lived out in everyday life in these early days of the twenty-first century. To all of us who are called by God to make a difference for good, this book is an inspiring instruction manual."

— Tony Campolo
Professor Emeritus, Eastern University

"It is easy to be overwhelmed by the vastness of need in our world today. But Max Lucado's accessible, encouraging, and powerful call to each of us to love Christ by loving those in need around us is a powerful gift to the church—it will enable us to begin the lives of meaning and significance for which God has created his people."

— Gary Haugen
President and CEO, International Justice Mission

"There has not been a clearer call to God's people to think strategically about world poverty while being challenged to act decisively. *Outlive Your Life* will ignite the passion for the poor that God desires to be found in each Christ follower."

— Dr. Barry Slauenwhite
President, Compassion Canada

"Max Lucado's deft and gentle look at the early church reveals us contemporary Christians as a sleepy, amnesiac people. We've forgotten our earthly purpose is to care, not for ourselves but for the poor and excluded. *Outlive Your Life* is a refreshing wake-up call, offering us a real sense of mission and our true identity as difference makers in a messed-up world."

— Greg Paul
sanctuarytoronto.ca; author, *The Twenty-Piece Shuffle* and *God in the Alley*

"With his trademark blend of lofty lyricism and earthy insight, Max Lucado artfully weaves together stories of hope—real-life accounts that incite and sustain the belief that change is possible through perhaps the unlikeliest of people—regular folk like you and me!"

— Jamie McIntosh
Founder and Executive Director,
International Justice Mission Canada

"God takes ordinary people to be his agents of transformation in the world and uses them in extraordinary ways. *Outlive Your Life* shows how this has happened in the past and applies it to the challenges now before us. It speaks to our God-given possibilities and shows a way to live that might change you forever."

— Tim Costello
CEO, World Vision Australia

"There has never been a better time for believers to show God's love, to sing His love to the nations. Thanks, Max, for reminding us that we each are designed to make a difference."

— Michael W. Smith
Best-Selling Christian music artist

"Max is a writer who disguises his genius well—he makes the most profound truth understandable to people like me. And then something miraculous happens. This truth changes your heart and, ultimately, somebody's else's world."

— Kathie Lee Gifford
Cohost, NBC's *The Today Show*

"My good friend Max Lucado never ceases to amaze me, and he has done it again! Reading *Outlive Your Life* inspires and encourages me to want to go out and help to change the world!"

— Mac Powell
Third Day

"Max Lucado is a living example of someone who most definitely will outlive his life because he has his eye on what people ultimately need: the Savior. Legacy—outliving your life—making your life count . . . there is no one more qualified to write about these things than Max Lucado."

— Dino Rizzo
Lead Pastor, Healing Place Church

"Max Lucado takes readers on a journey of generosity, justice, and caring. He challenges us to see the full gospel of Jesus at work in the lives of those who have and those who don't. *Outlive Your Life* is rich with stories of people whose love for their neighbors is only matched by their love for God. Max, you are right: we were made to make a difference."

— Dave Toycen
President and CEO, World Vision Canada

"One of my favorite communicators and one of my favorite topics. I love Max Lucado and was riveted, inspired, and blown away by *Outlive Your Life*. He makes the things we believe to be impossible not only do-able . . . but compelling."

— Mary Graham
Women of Faith®

"No one is better qualified to creatively inspire us to make a difference than Max Lucado. His call for a resurgence of compassion and service is compelling. For your legacy's sake I encourage you to read this book."

— Dave Wells
Chair, The Evangelical Fellowship of Canada

"Max Lucado has passionately discipled a generation in how to live out our faith. In *Outlive Your Life* he teaches us to live compassionately in our hurting world and reveals why God deliberately chooses ordinary people like you and me to carry out His mandate."

— Dr. Wess Stafford
President and CEO, Compassion
International

"With *Outlive Your Life* Max Lucado continues to add to his already amazing legacy. Once again Max helps reveal the heart of God in such an impactful way. You will be challenged and motivated."

— TobyMac
Grammy Award-winning recording artist

"Lucado shows fans both longtime and new that he remains, after all these years, a powerful voice in the call to authentic Christianity."

— *Publishers Weekly*

"Tens of millions have discovered Max Lucado, and God has used his books to touch deeply people of many tribes, nations, and languages. I celebrate Max's twenty-five years of published writing and am pleased to recommend—wholeheartedly and enthusiastically—both Max Lucado *and* his books!"

— Randy Alcorn
Author, *Heaven* and *If God Is Good*

One hundred percent of the author's royalties from
Outlive Your Life products will benefit children and
families through World Vision and
other ministries of faith-based compassion.
To follow World Vision's use
of the funds, go to
MaxLucado.com

INSPIRATIONAL

On the Anvil (1985)

No Wonder They Call Him the Savior (1986)

God Came Near (1987)

Six Hours One Friday (1989)

The Applause of Heaven (1990)

In the Eye of the Storm (1991)

And the Angels Were Silent (1992)

He Still Moves Stones (1993)

When God Whispers Your Name (1994)

A Gentle Thunder (1995)

In the Grip of Grace (1996)

The Great House of God (1997)

Just Like Jesus (1998)

When Christ Comes (1999)

He Chose the Nails (2000)

Traveling Light (2001)

A Love Worth Giving (2002)

Next Door Savior (2003)

Come Thirsty (2004)

It's Not About Me (2004)

Cure for the Common Life (2005)

Facing Your Giants (2006)

3:16 (2007)

Every Day Deserves a Chance (2007)

Cast of Characters (2008)

Fearless (2009)

Outlive Your Life (2010)

FICTION

An Angel's Story

The Christmas Candle

The Christmas Child

GIFT BOOKS

A Heart Like Jesus

Everyday Blessings

For These Tough Times

God's Mirror

God's Promises for You

God Thinks You're Wonderful

Grace for the Moment, Vol. 1 & II

Grace for the Moment Journal

In the Beginning

Just for You

Just Like Jesus Devotional

Let the Journey Begin

Max on Life Series

Mocha with Max

One Incredible Moment

Safe in the Shepherd's Arms

The Cross

The Gift for All People

The Greatest Moments

Traveling Light for Mothers

Traveling Light Journal

Turn

Walking with the Savior

You: God's Brand-New Idea!

BIBLES (GENERAL EDITOR)

Grace for the Moment Daily Bible

He Did This Just for You (New Testament)

The Devotional Bible

The Lucado Life Lessons Study Bible

OUTLIVE YOUR LIFE

You Were Made to Make a Difference

Max Lucado

THOMAS NELSON
Since 1798

NASHVILLE   DALLAS   MEXICO CITY   RIO DE JANEIRO

Published in Nashville, Tennessee, by Thomas Nelson. Thomas Nelson is a registered trademark of Thomas Nelson, Inc.

Thomas Nelson, Inc. titles may be purchased in bulk for educational, business, fund-raising, or sales promotional use. For information, please e-mail SpecialMarkets@ThomasNelson.com.

Unless otherwise noted, Scripture quotations are taken from the New King James Version®. © 1982 by Thomas Nelson, Inc. Used by permission. All rights reserved.

Scripture quotations marked CEV are from the Contemporary English Version. © 1991 by the American Bible Society. Used by permission.

Scripture quotations marked ESV are from the English Standard Version. © 2001 by Crossway Bibles, a division of Good News Publishers.

Scripture quotations marked KJV are from the King James Version.

Scripture quotations marked MSG are from *The Message* by Eugene H. Peterson. © 1993, 1994, 1995, 1996, 2000, 2001, 2002. Used by permission of NavPress Publishing Group.

Scripture quotations marked NCV are from the New Century Version®. © 2005 by Thomas Nelson, Inc. Used by permission. All rights reserved.

Scripture quotations marked NIV are from the Holy Bible, New International Version®, NIV®. © 1973, 1978, 1984 by Biblica, Inc.™ Used by permission of Zondervan. All rights reserved worldwide.

Scripture quotations marked NLT are from the Holy Bible, New Living Translation. © 1996, 2004. Used by permission of Tyndale House Publishers, Inc., Wheaton, Illinois 60189. All rights reserved.

Scripture quotations marked NRSV are from the New Revised Standard Version of the Bible. © 1989 by the Division of Christian Education of the National Council of the Churches of Christ in the U.S.A. All rights reserved.

Any italics in the Scripture quotations reflect the author's own emphasis.

ISBN 978-0-8499-4668-4 (IE)

Library of Congress Cataloging-in-Publication Data

Lucado, Max.
    Outlive your life : you were made to make a difference / Max Lucado.
       p. cm.
    Includes bibliographical references.
    ISBN 978-0-8499-2069-1 (hardcover)
     1. Christian life. I. Title.
BV4501.3.L856 2010
248.4—dc22   2010004014

Printed in the United States of America

10 11 12 13 14 WC 5 4 3 2 1

Denalyn and I would like to dedicate this book to my sister and brother-in-law,

Jacquelyn and Ken Wallace.

Kinder hearts may exist but not this side of heaven.

We love you.

Contents

Acknowledgments

Behind this book stands an army of thinkers, strategists, dreamers, and grinders.

Liz Heaney and Karen Hill—Editors who practiced CPR on this book and its author more than once. Astounding work!

Steve and Cheryl Green—Had you lived a century ago, you would have driven a herd of cattle to Montana. Nobody can keep a herd on the right trail the way you can.

Carol Bartley—Is your middle name Precision? Thank you for unleashing your skills on this book.

Mike Hyatt, David Moberg, Susan and Greg Ligon, Dave Schroeder, and the entire Thomas Nelson team—You set the standard for servanthood and excellence. Paula Major, welcome to the team!

Rich Stearns and the World Vision organization—You *must* keep speaking about the poor. They need your help, and we need your wake-up call.

Randy and Rozanne Frazee—You lift the heart of every person you meet! What a blend of intellect and kindness. So glad to be your partner.

David Drury and Greg Pruett—Tremendous insights from you both. You not only know the book of Acts; you live it.

David Treat—Your steady prayer is like a sturdy wall. Thank you for the cover.

The UpWords ministry team—For every phone and question you answer, way to go!

The Oak Hills Church—The best is yet to be!

Brett and Jenna Bishop, Andrea Lucado, and Sara Lucado—I am stunned by your faith and maturity. If pride were cookies, I'd be the bakery.

And Denalyn, my dear, dear wife—When God created the heavens and earth, the angels watched in silence. When he created you, they broke into applause. I hear them applauding still.

And to you, the reader—This book marks a milestone for me: twenty-five years in publishing. Thank you for encouraging me on this journey. And join me in thanking God. We all know the truth: he is the source of anything good. If my words have helped you, thank him that he still speaks through donkeys like me.

Finding Father Benjamin: A Fable

Unfavorable winds blow the ship off course, and when they do, the sailors spot uncharted islands. They see half a dozen mounds rising out of the blue South Seas waters. The captain orders the men to drop anchor and goes ashore. He is a robust man with a barrel chest, full beard, and curious soul.

On the first island he sees nothing but sadness. Underfed children. Tribes in conflict. No farming or food development, no treatment for the sick, and no schools. Just simple, needy people.

The second and following islands reveal more of the same. The captain sighs at what he sees. "This is no life for these people." But what can he do?

Then he steps onto the last and largest island. The people are healthy and well fed. Irrigation systems nourish their fields, and roads connect the villages. The children have bright eyes and strong bodies. The captain asks the chief for an explanation. How has this island moved so far ahead of the others?

The chief, who is smaller than the captain but every bit his equal in confidence, gives a quick response: "Father Benjamin. He educated us in everything from agriculture to health. He built schools and clinics and dug wells."

The captain asks, "Can you take me to see him?"

The chief nods and signals for two tribesmen to join him. They guide the captain over a jungle ridge to a simple, expansive medical clinic. It is equipped with clean beds and staffed with trained caretakers. They show the captain the shelves of medicine and introduce him to the staff. The captain, though impressed, sees nothing of Father Benjamin. He repeats his request. "I would like to see Father Benjamin. Can you take me to where he lives?"

The three natives look puzzled. They confer among themselves. After several minutes the chief invites, "Follow us to the other side of the island." They walk along the shoreline until they reach a series of fishponds. Canals connect the ponds to the ocean. As the tide rises, fish pass from the ocean into the ponds. The islanders then lower canal gates and trap the fish for harvest.

Again the captain is amazed. He meets fishermen and workers, gatekeepers and net casters. But he sees nothing of Father Benjamin. He wonders if he is making himself clear.

"I don't see Father Benjamin. Please take me to where he lives."

The trio talks alone again. After some discussion the chief offers, "Let's go up the mountain." They lead the captain up a steep, narrow path. After many twists and turns the path deposits them in front of a grass-roofed chapel. The voice of the chief is soft and earnest. "He has taught us about God."

He escorts the captain inside and shows him the altar, a large wooden cross, several rows of benches, and a Bible.

"Is this where Father Benjamin lives?" the captain asks.

The men nod and smile.

"May I talk to him?"

Their faces grow suddenly serious. "Oh, that would be impossible."

"Why?"

"He died many years ago."

The bewildered captain stares at the men. "I asked to see him, and you showed me a clinic, some fish farms, and this chapel. You said nothing of his death."

"You didn't ask about his death," the chief explains. "You asked to see where he lives. We showed you."

CHAPTER 1

Our Once-in-History Opportunity

By the time you knew what to call it, you were neck deep in it. You'd toddler-walked and talked, smelled crayons and swung bats, gurgled and giggled your way out of diapers and into childhood.

You'd noticed how guys aren't gals and dogs aren't cats and pizza sure beats spinach. And then, somewhere in the midst of it all, it hit you. At your grandpa's funeral perhaps. Maybe when you waved good-bye as your big brother left for the marines. You realized that these days are more than ice cream trips, homework, and pimples. This is called life. And this one is yours.

Complete with summers and songs and gray skies and tears, you have a life. Didn't request one, but you have one. A first day. A final day. And a few thousand in between. You've been given an honest-to-goodness human life.

You've been given *your* life. No one else has your version. You'll never bump into yourself on the sidewalk. You'll never meet anyone who has your exact blend of lineage, loves, and longings. Your life will never be lived by anyone else. You're not a jacket in an attic that can be recycled after you are gone.

And who pressed the accelerator? As soon as one day is lived, voilà, here comes another. The past has passed, and the good old days are exactly that: old days, the stuff of rearview mirrors and scrapbooks. Life is racing by, and if we aren't careful, you and I will look up, and our shot at it will have passed us by.

Some people don't bother with such thoughts. They grind through their days without lifting their eyes to look. They live and die and never ask why.

But you aren't numbered among them, or you wouldn't be holding a book entitled *Outlive Your Life*. It's not enough for you to do well. You want to do good. You want your life to matter. You want to live in such a way that the world will be glad you did.

But how can you? How can I? Can God use us?

I have one hundred and twenty answers to that question. One hundred and twenty residents of ancient Israel. They were the charter members of the Jerusalem church (Acts 1:15). Fishermen, some. Revenue reps, others. A former streetwalker and a converted revolutionary or two. They had no clout with Caesar, no friends at the temple headquarters. Truth be told, they had nothing more than this: a fire in the belly to change the world.

Thanks to Luke we know how they fared. He recorded their stories in the book of Acts. Let's listen to it. That's right—*listen* to the book of Acts. It cracks with the sounds of God's ever-expanding work. Press your ear against the pages, and hear God press into the corners and crevices of the world.

Hear sermons echo off the temple walls. Baptismal waters splashing, just-saved souls laughing. Hear the spoon scrape the bowl as yet another hungry mouth is fed.

Listen to the doors opening and walls collapsing. Doors to Antioch,

Ethiopia, Corinth, and Rome. Doors into palaces, prisons, and Roman courts.

And walls. The ancient prejudice between Jew and Samaritan—down! The thick and spiked division between Jew and Gentile—*crash!* The partitions that quarantine male from female, landowner from pauper, master from slave, black African from Mediterranean Jew—God demolishes them all.

Acts announces, "God is afoot!"

Is he still? we wonder. *Would God do with us what he did with his first followers?*

Heaven knows we hope so. These are devastating times: 1.75 billion people are desperately poor,[1] 1 billion are hungry,[2] millions are trafficked in slavery, and pandemic diseases are gouging entire nations. Each year nearly 2 million children are exploited in the global commercial sex trade.[3] And in the five minutes it took you to read these pages, almost ninety children died of preventable diseases.[4] More than half of all Africans do not have access to modern health facilities. As a result, 10 million of them die each year from diarrhea, acute respiratory illness, malaria, and measles. Many of those deaths could be prevented by one shot.[5]

Yet in the midst of the wreckage, here we stand, the modern-day version of the Jerusalem church. You, me, and our one-of-a-kind lifetimes and once-in-history opportunity.

Ours is the wealthiest generation of Christians ever. We are bright, educated, and experienced. We can travel around the world in twenty-four hours or send a message in a millisecond. We have the most sophisticated research and medicines at the tips of our fingers. We have ample resources. A mere 2 percent of the world's grain harvest would be enough, if shared, to erase the problems of hunger and malnutrition around the world.[6] There is enough food on the planet to offer every person twenty-five hundred calories of sustenance a day.[7] We have enough food to feed the hungry.

And we have enough bedrooms to house the orphans. Here's the math. There are 145 million orphans worldwide.[8] Nearly 236 million people in the United States call themselves Christians.[9] From a purely statistical standpoint, American Christians by themselves have the wherewithal to house every orphan in the world.

Of course, many people are not in a position to do so. They are elderly, infirm, unemployed, or simply feel no call to adopt. Yet what if a small percentage of them did? Hmmm, let's say 6 percent. If so, we could provide loving homes for the more than 14.1 million children in sub-Saharan Africa who have been orphaned by the AIDS epidemic.[10] Among the noble causes of the church, how does that one sound? "American Christians Stand Up for AIDS Orphans." Wouldn't that headline be a welcome one?

I don't mean to oversimplify these terribly complicated questions. We can't just snap our fingers and expect the grain to flow across borders or governments to permit foreign adoptions. Policies stalemate the best of efforts. International relations are strained. Corrupt officials snag the systems. I get that.

But this much is clear: the storehouse is stocked. The problem is not in the supply; the problem is in the distribution. God has given this generation, *our generation*, everything we need to alter the course of human suffering.

A few years back, three questions rocked my world. They came from different people in the span of a month. Question 1: Had you been a German Christian during World War II, would you have taken a stand against Hitler? Question 2: Had you lived in the South during the civil rights conflict, would you have taken a stand against racism? Question 3: When your grandchildren discover you lived during a day in which 1.75 billion people were poor and 1 billion were hungry, how will they judge your response?

I didn't mind the first two questions. They were hypothetical. I'd like to think I would have taken a stand against Hitler and fought against racism. But those days are gone, and those choices were not mine. But the third question has kept me awake at night. I do live today; so do you. We are given a choice . . . an opportunity to make a big difference during a difficult time. What if we did? What if we rocked the world with hope? Infiltrated all corners with God's love and life? What if we followed the example of the Jerusalem church? This tiny sect expanded into a world-changing force. We still drink from their wells and eat from their trees of faith. How did they do it? What can we learn from their priorities and passion?

Let's ponder their stories, found in the first twelve chapters of Acts. Let's examine each event through the lens of this prayer: *Do it again, Jesus. Do it again.* After all, "We are God's masterpiece. He has created us anew in Christ Jesus, so we can do the good things he planned for us long ago" (Eph. 2:10 NLT). We are created by a great God to do great works. He invites us to outlive our lives, not just in heaven but here on earth.

Here's a salute to a long life: goodness that outlives the grave, love that outlasts the final breath. May you live in such a way that your death is just the beginning of your life.

After David had done the will
of God in his own generation, he died and was buried.

(Acts 13:36 NLT)

O Lord, what an amazing opportunity you have spread out before me—a chance to make a difference for you in a desperately hurting world. Help me to see the needs you want me to see, to react in a way that honors you, and to bless others by serving them gladly with practical expressions of your love. Help me be Jesus' hands and feet, and through your Spirit give me the strength and wisdom I need to fulfill your plan for me in my own generation. In Jesus' name I pray, amen.

CHAPTER 2

Calling Mr. Pot Roast

You will be my witnesses in Jerusalem, and in all Judea and Samaria, and to the ends of the earth.

—ACTS 1:8 (NIV)

They don't look like much. No one has accused them of overqualification. Clumsiness, yes. Hardheadedness and forgetfulness, for certain. But ambassadors? Avant-garde leaders? Hope harbingers?

Not quite.

The tall one in the corner—that's Peter. Galilee thickened his accent. Fishing nets thickened his hands. Stubbornness thickened his skull. His biggest catch in life thus far has come with fins and gills. Odd. The guy pegged to lead the next great work of God knows more about bass and boat docks than he does about Roman culture or Egyptian leaders.

And his cronies: Andrew, James, Nathanael. Never traveled farther than a week's walk from home. Haven't studied the ways of Asia or the culture of Greece. Their passports aren't worn; their ways aren't sophisticated. Do they have any formal education?

In fact, what do they have? Humility? They jockeyed for cabinet positions. Sound theology? Peter told Jesus to forget the cross. Sensitivity? John wanted to torch the Gentiles. Loyalty? When Jesus needed prayers, they snoozed. When Jesus was arrested, they ran.

Thanks to their cowardice, Christ had more enemies than friends at his execution.

Yet look at them six weeks later, crammed into the second floor of a Jerusalem house, abuzz as if they'd just won tickets to the World Cup Finals. High fives and wide eyes. Wondering what in the world Jesus had in mind with his final commission: "You will be my witnesses in Jerusalem, and in all Judea and Samaria, and to the ends of the earth" (Acts 1:8 NIV).

You hillbillies will be my witnesses.

You uneducated and simple folk will be my witnesses.

You who once called me crazy, who shouted at me in the boat and doubted me in the Upper Room.

You temperamental, parochial net casters and tax collectors.

You will be my witnesses.

You will spearhead a movement that will explode like a just-opened fire hydrant out of Jerusalem and spill into the ends of the earth: into the streets of Paris, the districts of Rome, and the ports of Athens, Istanbul, Shanghai, and Buenos Aires. You will be a part of something so mighty, controversial, and head spinning that two millennia from now a middle-aged, redheaded author riding in the exit row of a flight from Boston to Dallas will type this question on his laptop:

Does Jesus still do it?

Does he still use simple folks like us to change the world? We suffer from such ordinariness. The fellow to my right snoozes with his mouth open. The gray-haired woman next to him wears earphones and bobs her head from side to side. (I think I hear Frank Sinatra.) They don't wear halos or wings. And excluding the reflection off the man's bald spot, they don't emit any light.

Most of us don't. We are Joe Pot Roast. Common folk. We sit in the bleachers, eat at diners, change diapers, and wear our favorite team's ball cap. Fans don't wave when we pass. Servants don't scurry when we come home. Chauffeurs don't drive our cars; butlers don't open our doors or draw our baths. Doormen don't greet us, and security doesn't protect us. We, like the Jerusalem disciples, are regular folk.

Does God use the common Joe?

Edith would say yes.

Edith Hayes was a spry eighty-year-old with thinning white hair, a wiry five-foot frame, and an unquenchable compassion for South Florida's cancer patients. I was fresh out of seminary in 1979 and sitting in an office of unpacked books when she walked in and introduced herself: "My name is Edith, and I help cancer patients." She extended her hand. I offered a chair. She politely declined. "Too busy. You'll see my team here at the church building every Tuesday morning. You're welcome to come, but if you come, we'll put you to work."

Her team, I came to learn, included a hundred or so silver-haired women who occupied themselves with the unglamorous concern of sore seepage. They made cancer wounds their mission, stitching together truckloads of disposable pads each Tuesday, then delivering them to patients throughout the week.

Edith rented an alley apartment, lived on her late husband's pension, wore glasses that magnified her pupils, and ducked applause like artillery fire. She would have fit in well with Peter and the gang.

So would Joe and Liz Page. Their battalion has a different objective—clothing for premature infants. They turn one of our church classrooms into a factory of volunteer seamstresses. The need for doll-sized wardrobes had never occurred to me. But then again, my children weren't born weighing only three pounds. Joe and Liz make sure such kids have something to wear, even if they wear it to their own funerals.

Joe retired from military service. Liz once taught school. He has heart problems. She has foot deformities. But both have a fire in their hearts for the neediest of children.

As does Caleb. He's nine years old. He plays basketball, avoids girls, and wants the kids of El Salvador to have clean drinking water.

During a Sunday school class, his teacher shared the reality of life in poverty-stricken Central America. For lack of clean drinking water, children die of preventable diseases every day. Caleb was stunned at the thought and stepped into action. He took the twenty dollars he had been saving for a new video game, gave it to the cause, and asked his father to match it. He then challenged the entire staff of the children's ministry at his church to follow his example. The result? Enough money to dig two wells in El Salvador.

Edith, Joe, Liz, and Caleb are regular folks. They don't levitate when they walk or see angels when they pray. They don't have a seat at the United Nations or a solution for the suffering in Darfur. But they do embrace this conviction: God doesn't call the qualified. He qualifies the called.

Don't let Satan convince you otherwise. He will try. He will tell you that God has an IQ requirement or an entry fee. That he employs only specialists and experts, governments and high-powered personalities. When Satan whispers such lies, dismiss him with this truth: God stampeded the first-century society with swaybacks, not thoroughbreds. Before Jesus came along, the disciples were loading trucks, coaching soccer, and selling Slurpee drinks at the convenience store. Their collars were blue, and their hands were calloused, and there is no evidence that Jesus chose them because they were smarter or nicer than the guy next door. The one thing they had going for them was a willingness to take a step when Jesus said, "Follow me."

Are you more dinghy than cruise ship? More stand-in than movie star? More plumber than executive? More blue jeans than blue blood? Congratulations. God changes the world with folks like you.

Just ask the twenty-two people who traveled to London on a fall morning in 2009 to thank Nicholas Winton. They could have passed for a retirement-home social club. All were in their seventies or eighties. More gray hair than not. More shuffled steps than quick ones.

But this was no social trip. It was a journey of gratitude. They came to thank the man who had saved their lives: a stooped centenarian who met them on a train platform just as he had in 1939.

He was a twenty-nine-year-old stockbroker at the time. Hitler's armies were ravaging the nation of Czechoslovakia, tearing Jewish families apart and marching parents to concentration camps. No one was caring for the children. Winton got wind of their plight and resolved to help them. He used his vacation to travel to Prague, where he met parents who, incredibly, were willing to entrust their children's future to his care. After returning to England, he worked his regular job on the stock exchange by day and advocated for the children at night. He convinced Great Britain to permit their entry. He found foster homes and raised funds. Then he scheduled his first transport on March 14, 1939, and accomplished seven more over the next five months. His last trainload of children arrived on August 2, bringing the total of rescued children to 669.

On September 1, the biggest transport was to take place, but

Hitler invaded Poland, and Germany closed borders throughout Europe. None of the 250 children on that train were ever seen again.

After the war Winton didn't tell anyone of his rescue efforts, not even his wife. In 1988 she found a scrapbook in their attic with all the children's photos and a complete list of names. She prodded him to tell the story. As he has, rescued children have returned to say thank you. The grateful group includes a film director, a Canadian journalist, a news correspondent, a former minister in the British cabinet, a magazine manager, and one of the founders of the Israeli Air Force. There are some seven thousand children, grandchildren, and great-grandchildren who owe their existence to Winton's bravery. He wears a ring given to him by some of the children he saved. It bears a line from the Talmud, the book of Jewish law: "Save one life. Save the world."[1]

Chalk up another one for the common guy.

Remember, dear brothers and sisters, that few of you were wise in the world's eyes or powerful or wealthy when God called you. Instead, God chose things the world considers foolish in order to shame those who think they are wise. And he chose things that are powerless to shame those who are powerful.

(1 Cor. 1:26–27 NLT)

Loving Father, you made me, so you know very well that I am but dust. Yet you have called me into your kingdom to serve you at this specific place, at this specific time, for a very specific purpose. Despite my ordinariness, I belong to you—and you are anything but ordinary! Help me pour out your grace and compassion upon others that they, too, may experience the richness of your love. Through me, my Father, show others how you can use an ordinary life to bring extraordinary blessing into the world. In Jesus' name I pray, amen.

CHAPTER 3

Let God Unshell You

They're speaking our languages,
describing God's mighty works!

—ACTS 2:11 (MSG)

May I show you my new clamshell? It just arrived. My old one was thinning out. You know how worn they can get. Sheer as the wall of a cheap motel. Mine was so chipped I could see right through it. And noise? It couldn't block the sound of a baby's whimper.

So I bought this new model. Special-ordered. Tailor-made. Top-of-the-line. I can stand up in it. Sit down in it. Sleep in the thing if I want to. Go ahead, take a look inside. See the flip-down ledge on the left? Cup holder! Check out the headphones. As if the shell's insulation wasn't enough, I can turn up the music and tune out the world. All I do is step in, grab the handle on the interior of the upper shell, and pull it closed.

Better than body armor, thick as an army tank. Think of it as a bunker for the soul. In here the world has no hunger or orphans. And poverty? This shell comes factory coated with a sadness screen. Racism? Injustice? They bounce off my shell like rain off a turtle's back.

Let me tell you how good this baby is. I went to the convenience store this morning for coffee and a paper. I was standing in the checkout line, minding my own business, when I noticed the fellow in front of me was paying with food stamps. He wore a baseball cap, baggy khakis, and flip-flops and had three kids at his knees. Close enough to detect his thick accent, I pegged him as an immigrant. I can typically stir up a good smirk and pigeonhole these people as fast as you can say, "Burden on society." But this family started getting to me. The little girls were strawberry sweet, with their skin the color of milk chocolate and their almond-shaped eyes. One of them smiled in my direction. Before I knew it, I smiled back.

About that time the cashier shook her head and returned the food stamps. Apparently their value wasn't enough to cover the purchase. The father gave her a confused look. That's when it hit me. *I can help him out.* Little did I know, a cloud of kindness vapor had been released into the store. My body began to react. A lump formed in my throat. Moisture puddled in the corners of my eyes. I began to experience a sensation in my chest: *gelatinous cardiacinus*, better known as soft heart.

Then came the involuntary reflexes. My left hand lifted to signal my willingness. The other dug in my pocket for money. That's when I snapped to my senses and realized what was happening. I was under a compassion attack. I immediately lifted the lid of my shell and climbed in. I noticed other shoppers had already taken cover. I barely escaped. What would we have done without our clamshells?

Don't know what I'd do without mine. When news reports describe Afghan refugees, into the shell I go. When a homeless person appears with a cardboard sign, I just close the lid. When missionaries describe multitudes of lost, lonely souls, I climb in. Why, just last week someone told me about regions of the world that have no clean water. Without my clamshell to protect me, who knows what I would have done. I might have written a check!

This is quite a shield. You probably have your own. Most of us have learned to insulate ourselves against the hurt of the hurting.

Haven't we? *Mustn't* we? After all, what can we do about the famine in Sudan, the plight of the unemployed, or a pandemic of malaria?

Clamshells. We come by them honestly. We don't intend to retreat from the world or stick our heads in a hole. We want to help. But the problems are immense (Did you say one billion are poor?), complex (When is helping actually hurting?), and intense (I have enough problems of my own.).

That's true. We do have our own issues. Our sputtering marriages, fading ambitions, dwindling bank accounts, and stubborn hearts. How can we change the world when we can't even change our bad habits? We don't have what it takes to solve these problems. Best to climb in and shut the shell, right?

You would have had a hard time selling that strategy to the Jerusalem church. Not after God unshelled them on the Day of Pentecost.

Pentecost was the busiest day of the year in Jerusalem—one of three feast days that all Jewish men, at some point in their lifetimes, were required to appear in the city. They traveled from Europe, Asia, and Africa. It's difficult to know the population of ancient cities, but some suggest that during this season Jerusalem swelled from a hundred thousand to a million inhabitants.[1] Her narrow streets ran thick with people of all shades of skin, from Ethiopian ebony to Roman olive. A dozen dialects bounced off the stone walls, and the temple treasury overflowed with every coin and currency.

Then there were the locals. The butcher and his meat. The wool comber and his loom. The shoemaker, hammering sandals. The tailor, plying his needle. White-robed priests and unsightly beggars. Every element of humanity crammed within the three hundred acres of the City of David.[2]

And somewhere in their midst, Jesus' followers were gathered in prayer. "When the Day of Pentecost had fully come, they were all with one accord in one place" (Acts 2:1). This is the earliest appearance of the church. Consider where God placed his people. Not isolated in a desert or quarantined in a bunker. Not separated from society, but smack-dab in the center of it, in the heart of one of the largest cities at its busiest time. And then, once he had them where he needed them . . .

> Suddenly there came a sound from heaven, as of a rushing mighty wind, and it filled the whole house where they were sitting. Then there appeared to them divided tongues, as of fire, and one sat upon each of them. And they were all filled with the Holy Spirit and began to speak with other tongues, as the Spirit gave them utterance. (vv. 2–4)

The Holy Spirit came upon them *suddenly*—not predictably or expectedly or customarily but suddenly. Welcome to the world of Acts and the "sudden" Spirit of God, sovereign and free, never subordinate to timing or technique. He creates his own agenda, determines his own calendar, and keeps his own hours.

Fire and wind now. House shaking later. Visiting the Samaritans after water baptism. Falling on the Gentiles before water baptism. And here, roaring like a tornado through Jerusalem. "[The sound] filled the whole house" (v. 2) and spilled into the streets. The whistling, rushing, blowing sound of a wind.

The Spirit came, first as wind, then appeared as individual tongues of fire, "and one sat upon each of them" (v. 3). This wasn't one torch over the entire room but individual flames hovering above each person.

And then the most unexpected thing happened.

[They] began to speak with other tongues, as the Spirit gave them utterance.

And there were dwelling in Jerusalem Jews, devout men, from every nation under heaven. And when this sound occurred, the multitude came together, and were confused, because everyone heard them speak in his own language. Then they were all amazed and marveled, saying to one another, "Look, are not all these who speak Galileans? And how is it that we hear, each in our own language in which we were born? Parthians and Medes and Elamites, those dwelling in Mesopotamia, Judea and Cappadocia, Pontus and Asia, Phrygia and Pamphylia, Egypt and the parts of Libya adjoining Cyrene, visitors from Rome, both Jews and proselytes, Cretans and Arabs—we hear them speaking in our own tongues the wonderful works of God." So they were all amazed and perplexed, saying to one another, "Whatever could this mean?" (vv. 4–12)

Envision such a phenomenon. Imagine a cosmopolitan center such as New York City. Fifth Avenue is packed with businesspeople, laborers, and travelers from all over the world. Early one morning as the mobs throb their way to work, the sound of a wind shakes the boulevard. The roar is so stout and robust that people stop dead in their tracks as if expecting to see a train blaze down the avenue. Taxi and bus drivers brake. Silence falls on the city only to be interrupted by the voices of a group gathered in Central Park. One hundred and twenty people speak, each one standing beneath a different flame, each one proclaiming God's goodness in a different language. Witnesses hear their native tongues. José, from Spain, hears about God's mercy in Spanish. Mako, from Japan, hears a message in Japanese. The group from the Philippines discerns

Tagalog. They hear different languages but one message: the wonders of God.

Oh to have heard this moment in Jerusalem. Andrew describing God's grace in Egyptian. Thomas explaining God's love to the Romans. Bartholomew quoting the Twenty-third Psalm to Cretans. John relating the resurrection story to the Cappadocians.

Some in the crowd were cynical, accusing the disciples of early-morning inebriation. But others were amazed and asked, "Whatever could this mean?" (v. 12).

Good question. Crowded city. Prayerful followers. Rushing wind and falling fire. Fifteen nations represented in one assembly. Disciples speaking like trained translators of the United Nations. Whatever could this mean?

At least this much: God loves the nations. He loves Iraqis. Somalians. Israelis. New Zealanders. Hondurans. He has a white-hot passion to harvest his children from every jungle, neighborhood, village, and slum. "*All the earth* shall be filled with the glory of the LORD" (Num. 14:21 ESV). During the days of Joshua, God brought his people into Canaan "so that *all the peoples of the earth* may know that the hand of the LORD is mighty" (Josh. 4:24 ESV). David commanded us to "sing to the LORD, *all the earth*! . . . Declare his glory among the nations, his marvelous works among *all the peoples*!" (Ps. 96:1–3 ESV). God spoke to us through Isaiah: "I will make you as a light for the nations, that my salvation may reach to the *end of the earth*" (Isa. 49:6 ESV). His vision for the end of history includes "people for God from *every* tribe, language, people, and nation" (Rev. 5:9 NCV).

God longs to proclaim his greatness in all 6,909 languages that exist in the world today.[3] He loves subcultures: the gypsies of Turkey, the hippies of California, the cowboys and rednecks of West Texas.

He has a heart for bikers and hikers, tree huggers and academics. Single moms. Gray-flanneled executives. He loves all people groups and equips us to be his voice. He commissions common Galileans, Nebraskans, Brazilians, and Koreans to speak the languages of the peoples of the world. He teaches us the vocabulary of distant lands, the dialect of the discouraged neighbor, the vernacular of the lonely heart, and the idiom of the young student. God outfits his followers to cross cultures and touch hearts.

Pentecost makes this promise: if you are in Christ, God's Spirit will speak through you.

Let God unshell you. And when he does, "make a careful exploration of who you are and the work you have been given, and then sink yourself into that" (Gal. 6:4 MSG). Don't miss the opportunity to discover your language.

With whom do you feel most fluent? Teenagers? Drug addicts? The elderly? You may be tongue-tied around children but eloquent with executives. This is how God designed you. "God has given us different gifts for doing certain things well" (Rom. 12:6 NLT).

For whom do you feel most compassion? God doesn't burden us equally.[4] "The LORD looks from heaven; He sees all the sons of men . . . *He fashions their hearts individually*" (Ps. 33:13, 15). When does your heart break and pulse race? When you spot the homeless? When you travel to the inner city? Or when you see the victims of sex trade in Cambodia? This was the tragedy that broke the hearts of three American women.

Ernstena is a pastor's wife. Clara is a businesswoman. Jo Anne had just started a small relief organization. They traveled to Cambodia to encourage Jim-Lo, a missionary friend. He led them to a section of his city where the modern sex trade runs rampant. An estimated fifteen thousand girls were on sale. At the time more than a hundred thousand young women in Cambodia had been sold into forced prostitution. Jo Anne, Clara, Ernstena, and Jim-Lo looked into the faces of teen girls, even preteens, and could see a devastating story in each. They began to snap pictures until the sellers threatened to take the camera away. The Christians had no idea what to do but pray.

The seedy avenue became their Upper Room. *Lord, what do you want us to do? It's so overwhelming.* They wept.

God heard their prayer and gave them their tools. Upon returning to the United States, Jo Anne wrote an article about the experience, which prompted a reader to send a great deal of money. With this gift the women formed an anti-trafficking ministry of World Hope International and provided housing for the young girls who were rescued or escaped from the brothels and sales stations. In just three years, four hundred children, ranging in age from two to fifteen, were rescued.

When the U.S. State Department sponsored an event called "The Salute to the 21st Century Abolitionists," they honored World Hope. They even asked one of the women to offer a prayer. The prayer that began on a Cambodian street continued in front of some of the most influential government officials in the world.[5]

Amazing what happens when we get out of our shells.

[God] comforts us in all our troubles so that we can comfort others. When they are troubled, we will be able to give them the same comfort God has given us.

(2 Cor. 1:4 NLT)

Gracious Father, you took the initiative to reach out to me—even in my sin and selfishness—in order to bring me into your eternal kingdom, through the work of Christ. I cannot fathom such love! And yet, Father, I try to hoard your grace! Put up walls of protection that I might keep hurt out and blessing in. I am like the clam that shuts itself up in its shell, afraid of threats from the outside. You call me to unshell myself and to partner with you in your mission of love. Unshell me, Lord, that I, too, may reach out to a lonely, discouraged, and even hopeless world. In Jesus' name, amen.

CHAPTER 4

Don't Forget the Bread

Your sins will be forgiven. Then you will be given the
Holy Spirit. This promise is for you.

—ACTS 2:38–39 (CEV)

Denalyn called as I was driving home the other day. "Can you stop at the grocery store and pick up some bread?"

"Of course."

"Do I need to tell you where to find it?"

"Are you kidding? I was born with a bread-aisle tracking system."

"Just stay focused, Max."

She was nervous. Rightly so. I am the *Exxon Valdez* of grocery shopping. My mom once sent me to buy butter and milk; I bought buttermilk. I mistook a tube of hair cream for toothpaste. I thought the express aisle was a place to express your opinion. I am a charter member of the Clueless Husband Shopping Squad. I can relate to the fellow who came home from the grocery store with one carton of eggs, two sacks of flour, three boxes of cake mix, four sacks of sugar, and five cans of cake frosting. His wife looked at the sacks of groceries and lamented, "I never should have numbered the list."

So, knowing that Denalyn was counting on me, I parked the car at the market and entered the door. En route to the bread aisle, I spotted my favorite cereal, so I picked up a box, which made me wonder if we needed milk. I found a gallon in the dairy section. The cold milk stirred images of one of God's great gifts to humanity: Oreo cookies. The heavenly banquet will consist of tables and tables of Oreo cookies and milk. We will spend eternity dipping and slurping our way through . . . Okay, enough of that.

I grabbed a pack of cookies, which happened to occupy the same half of the store as barbecue potato chips. What a wonderful world this is—cookies and barbecue chips under the same roof! On the way to the checkout counter, I spotted some ice cream. Within a few minutes I'd filled the basket with every essential item for a happy and fulfilled life. I checked out and drove home.

Denalyn looked at my purchases, then at me. Can you guess her question? All together now: "Where's the bread?"

I went back to the grocery store.

I forgot the big item. The one thing I went to get. The one essential product. I forgot the bread.

Might we make the same mistake in a more critical arena? In an effort to do good, we can get distracted. We feed people. We encourage, heal, help, and serve. We address racial issues and poverty. Yet there is one duty we must fulfill. We can't forget the bread.

Peter didn't.

Now, listen to what I have to say about Jesus from Nazareth. God proved that he sent Jesus to you by having him work miracles, wonders, and signs. All of you know this. God had already planned and decided that Jesus would be handed over to you. So you took him and had evil men put him to death on a cross. But God set him free from death and raised him to life. Death could not hold him in its power. (Acts 2:22–24 CEV)

Peter was responding to the question of the people: "Whatever could this mean?" (2:12). The sound of rushing wind, the images of fire, the sudden linguistic skills of the disciples . . . whatever could these occurrences mean? He positioned himself over the plaza full of people and proceeded to introduce the crowd to Jesus. Jerusalemites had surely heard of Jesus. He was the subject of a headline-grabbing trial and execution seven weeks before. But did they *know* Jesus? In rapid succession Peter fired a trio of God-given endorsements of Christ.

1. "God proved that he sent Jesus to you by having him work miracles, wonders, and signs" (v. 22 CEV).

   Jesus' miracles were proof of his divinity. When he healed bodies and fed hungry bellies, when he commanded the waves as casually as a four-star general does the private, when he called life out of Lazarus's dead body and sight out of the blind man's eyes, these miracles were God's endorsement. God gave Jesus his seal of approval.

2. Then God delivered him to death. "[He] had already planned and decided that Jesus would be handed over to you. So you took him and had evil men put him to death on a cross" (v. 23 CEV).

   God deemed Christ worthy of God's most important mission—to serve as a sacrifice for humankind. Not just anyone could do this. How could a sinner die for sinners? Impossible. The Lamb of God had to be perfect, flawless, and sinless. When the Romans nailed Jesus to the cross, God was singling him out as the only sinless being ever to walk the face of the earth, the only person qualified to bear "our sins in His own body" (1 Peter 2:24). The cross, a tool of shame, was actually a badge of honor, a badge bestowed one time, to one man, Jesus of Nazareth. But God did not leave Jesus in the tomb.

3. "God set him free from death and raised him to life. Death could not hold him in its power" (Acts 2:24 CEV).

Deep within the dark sepulchre of Joseph of Arimathea, behind the secured and sealed rock of the Romans, amid the sleeping corpses and silent graves of the Jews, God did his greatest work. He spoke to the dead body of his incarnate Son. With hell's demons and heaven's angels watching, he called on the Rose of Sharon to lift his head, the Lion of Judah to stretch his paws, the Bright and Morning Star to shine forth his light, the Alpha and Omega to be the beginning of life and the end of the grave. "God untied the death ropes and raised him up. Death was no match for him" (v. 24 MSG).

I envision Peter pausing at this point in his sermon. I can hear words echo off the Jerusalem stones. "Death was no match for him . . . for him . . . for him." Then for a few seconds, hushed quiet. Peter stops and searches the faces, his dark eyes defying someone to challenge his claim. A priest, a soldier, a cynic—someone, anyone, to question his words. "You are insane, Simon. Come, let me take you to Joseph of Arimathea's tomb. Let's roll back the stone and unwrap the decaying cadaver of Jesus and put an end to this nonsense once and for all."

What an opportunity for someone to destroy Christianity in its infancy! But no one defied Peter. No Pharisee objected. No soldier protested. No one spoke, because no one had the body. The word was out that the Word was out.

People began to realize their mistake. The gravity of their crime settled over them like a funeral dirge. God came into their world, and they killed him. This was the thrust of Peter's sermon: "*You killed God.*" "God proved . . . to you . . . All of you know this . . . You took him and had evil men put him to death." You. You. You. On three occasions Peter pointed a verbal, if not physical, finger at the crowd.

The question of the hour changed. "Whatever could this mean?" (a question of the head) became "What shall we do?" (a question of the heart). "Men and brethren, what shall we do?" (v. 37).

They leaned in to hear Peter's reply. So much was at stake. What if he said, "It's too late"? Or "You had your chance"? Or "You should have listened the first time"?

Peter, surely with outstretched arms and tear-filled eyes, gave this invitation:

> Turn back to God! Be baptized in the name of Jesus Christ, so that your sins will be forgiven. Then you will be given the Holy Spirit. This promise is for you and your children. It is for everyone our Lord God will choose, no matter where they live. (vv. 38–39 CEV)

Peter would eventually speak about poverty. The church would soon address the issues of widows, disease, and bigotry. But not yet. The first order of the church's first sermon was this: pardon for all our sins. Peter delivered the bread.

Would you allow me to do the same? Before we turn the next

page in the story of Acts, would you consider the offer of Jesus? "I am the bread of life. Whoever comes to me will never be hungry again" (John 6:35 NLT).

The grain-to-bread process is a demanding one. The seed must be planted before it can grow. When the grain is ripe, it must be cut down and ground into flour. Before it can become bread, it must pass through the oven. Bread is the end result of planting, harvesting, and heating.

Jesus endured an identical process. He was born into this world. He was cut down, bruised, and beaten on the threshing floor of Calvary. He passed through the fire of God's wrath, for our sake. He "suffered because of others' sins, the Righteous One for the unrighteous ones. He went through it all—was put to death and then made alive—to bring us to God" (1 Peter 3:18 MSG).

Bread of Life? Jesus lived up to the title. But an unopened loaf does a person no good. Have you received the bread? Have you received God's forgiveness?

We cherish pardon, don't we? I was thinking about pardon a few afternoons ago on a south Texas country road with hills and curves and turns and bends. I know it well. I now know the highway patrolman who oversees it.

And he now knows me. He looked at my driver's license. "Why is your name familiar to me? Aren't you a minister here in San Antonio?"

"Yes, sir."

"On your way to a funeral?"

"No."

"An emergency?"

"No."

"You were going awfully fast."

"I know."

"Tell you what I'm going to do. I'm going to give you a second chance."

I sighed. "Thank you. And thanks for giving me a sermon illustration on pardon."

God has posted his traffic signs everywhere we look. In the universe, in Scripture, even within our own hearts. Yet we persist in disregarding his directions. But God does not give us what we deserve. He has drenched his world in grace. It has no end. It knows no limits. It empowers this life and enables us to live the next. God offers second chances, like a soup kitchen offers meals to everyone who asks.

And that includes you. Make sure you receive the bread.

And once you do, pass it on. After all, if we don't, who will? Governments don't feed the soul. The secular relief house can give a bed, a meal, and valuable counsel. But we can give much more. Not just help for this life but hope for the next.

> Turn back to God! Be baptized in the name of Jesus Christ, so that your sins will be forgiven. Then you will be given the Holy Spirit. This promise is for you and your children. It is for everyone our Lord God will choose, no matter where they live. (Acts 2:38–39 CEV)

So along with the cups of water, plates of food, and vials of medicine, let there be the message of sins forgiven and death defeated.

Remember the bread.

For God was in Christ, reconciling the world to himself, no longer counting people's sins against them. And he gave us this wonderful message of reconciliation. So we are Christ's ambassadors; God is making his appeal through us. We speak for Christ when we plead, "Come back to God!" For God made Christ, who never sinned, to be the offering for our sin, so that we could be made right with God through Christ.

(2 Cor. 5:19–21 NLT)

My blessed Savior and Lord, I praise you for freely giving me the Bread of Life. You replaced my darkness with your light, my fear with your security, and my despair with your hope. Remind me every day, Father, that the Bread of Life I have in Jesus comes to me by your grace and through your love—and that it delights your generous heart when I tell others where they can find and partake. Make me into an eager ambassador of Jesus Christ. Turn my fear into boldness so that heaven's streets may be filled with men and women who love the Savior, in part because they first heard of his grace and mercy from my lips. In Jesus' name I pray, amen.

CHAPTER 5

Team Up

Now all who believed were together.

—ACTS 2:44

In 1976 tremors devastated the highlands of Guatemala. Thousands of people were killed, and tens of thousands were left homeless. A philanthropist offered to sponsor a relief team from our college. This flyer was posted in our dormitory: "Needed: students willing to use their spring break to build cinder-block homes in Quetzaltenango." I applied, was accepted, and began attending the orientation sessions.

There were twelve of us in all. Mostly ministry students. All of us, it seemed, loved to discuss theology. We were young enough in our faith to believe we knew all the answers. This made for lively discussions. We bantered about a covey of controversies. I can't remember the list. It likely included the usual suspects of charismatic gifts, end times, worship styles, and church strategy. By the time we reached Guatemala, we'd covered the controversies and revealed our true colors. I'd discerned the faithful from the infidels, the healthy from the heretics. I knew who was in and who was out.

But all of that was soon forgotten. The destruction from the earthquake dwarfed our differences. Entire villages had been leveled. Children were wandering through rubble. Long lines of wounded people awaited medical attention. Our opinions seemed suddenly petty. The disaster demanded teamwork. The challenge created a team.

The task turned rivals into partners. I remember one fellow in particular. He and I had distinctly different opinions regarding the styles of worship music. I—the open-minded, relevant thinker—favored contemporary, upbeat music. He—the stodgy, close-minded caveman—preferred hymns and hymnals. Yet when stacking bricks for houses, guess who worked shoulder to shoulder? As we did, we began to sing together. We sang old songs and new, slow and fast. Only later did the irony of it dawn on me. Our common concern gave us a common song.

This was Jesus' plan all along. None of us can do what all of us can do. Remember his commission to the disciples? "You [all of you collectively] will be my witnesses" (Acts 1:8 NIV). Jesus didn't issue individual assignments. He didn't move one by one down the line and knight each individual.

"You, Peter, will be my witness . . ."

"You, John, will be my witness . . ."

"You, Mary Magdalene, will be my witness . . ."

But rather, "You [the sum of you] will be my witnesses . . ." Jesus works in community. For that reason you find no personal pronouns in the earliest description of the church:

> All the believers devoted themselves to the apostles' teaching, and to fellowship, and to sharing in meals (including the Lord's Supper), and to prayer.
>
> A deep sense of awe came over them all, and the apostles performed many miraculous signs and wonders. And all the believers met together in one place and shared everything they had. They

sold their property and possessions and shared the money with those in need. They worshiped together at the Temple each day, met in homes for the Lord's Supper, and shared their meals with great joy. (Acts 2:42–46 NLT)

The cameo contains only plural nouns and pronouns.

"All the *believers*."

"Devoted *themselves*."

"Awe came over *them* all."

"All the *believers* met together . . . and shared everything."

"*They* sold *their* property and possessions and shared."

"*They* worshiped together . . . and shared *their* meals."

No *I* or *my* or *you*. We are in this together. We are more than followers of Christ, disciples of Christ. "We are parts of his body" (Eph. 5:30 NCV). "He is the head of the body, which is the church" (Col. 1:18 NCV). I am not his body; you are not his body. We—together—are his body.

But his body has been known to misbehave. The brain discounts the heart. (Academics discount worshippers.) The hands criticize the knees. (People of action criticize people of prayer.) The eyes refuse to partner with the feet. (Visionary thinkers won't work with steady laborers.)

A clear case of mutiny on the body.

If the foot should say, "Because I am not a hand, I am not of the body," is it therefore not of the body? And if the ear should say, "Because I am not an eye, I am not of the body," is it therefore not of the body? If the whole body were an eye, where would be the hearing? If the whole were hearing, where would be the smelling? But

now God has set the members, each one of them, in the body just as
He pleased. (1 Cor. 12:15–18)

The early Christians surely chuckled at these word pictures. What
if the whole body were an eye? If you were a collection of eyeballs,
how would you function? Five eyes on your hand, which is an eye,
attached to your arm-sized eye, affixed to a torso eye from which
extends your neck eye, and . . . The thought is ludicrous! You'd
have to bathe in Visine. But, then again, you couldn't bathe, for you
wouldn't have hands.

"The eye cannot say to the hand, 'I have no need of you'" (v. 21).

We cannot say, "I have no need of you." The megachurch needs
the smaller church. The liberal needs the conservative. The pastor
needs the missionary. Cooperation is more than a good idea; it is a
command. "Make every effort to keep the unity of the Spirit through
the bond of peace" (Eph. 4:3 NIV). Unity matters to God. There is
"one flock and one shepherd" (John 10:16 NIV).

What if the missing ingredient for changing the world is teamwork? "When two of you get together on anything at all on earth
and make a prayer of it, my Father in heaven goes into action. And
when two or three of you are together because of me, you can be sure
that I'll be there" (Matt. 18:19–20 MSG).

This is an astounding promise. When believers agree, Jesus takes
notice, shows up, and hears our prayers.

And when believers disagree? Can we return to my Guatemalan
memory for a moment?

Suppose our group had clustered according to opinions. Divided
according to doctrines. If we had made unanimity a prerequisite for
partnership, can you imagine the consequences? We wouldn't have

accomplished anything. When workers divide, it is the suffering who suffer most.

They've suffered enough, don't you think? The Jerusalem church found a way to work together. They found common ground in the death, burial, and resurrection of Christ. Because they did, lives were changed.

And as you and I do, the same will happen.

We will help more and more people, such as José Ferreira. He runs a small pharmacy in a slum of Rio de Janeiro, Brazil. It's really more a tin-walled shed and bench, but since he sells medicine, it bears the hand-painted sign Farmácia. He started his store with three dollars' worth of medical supplies that he bought from a larger pharmacy downtown. As soon as he sells the medicine, he closes his store, walks to a nearby bus stop, rides one hour to the larger pharmacy, and buys more stock.

By the time he returns, it is dark, so he waits until the next morning and repeats the cycle: open, sell the product, close the store, and travel to purchase inventory. Some days he does this twice. Since his store is closed as much as it is open, he scarcely makes a profit. He and his family live in the back of the shack and subsist on the equivalent of three dollars a day. If rains flood the favela and wash away his shack, he will lose everything. If one of his children comes down with dengue fever, he likely will not have the money for medicine. José knows this. But what can he do? He indwells the low-ceilinged world of the poor.

But while José is struggling in Rio, God is working in London. A good-hearted taxi driver named Thomas reads an article in a magazine. It details the fascinating process of microfinance. Microfinance provides small loans to poor people so they can increase their income and decrease their vulnerability to unforeseen circumstances. Thomas is not rich, but he is blessed. He would happily help a fellow businessperson on the other side of the world. But how can he? Can a British taxi driver help a Brazilian merchant? Through microfinance organizations, he can.

So he does.

A few days later José is offered a microloan of fifty-five dollars. In order to qualify for it, however, he has to join a borrower group of six neighboring businessmen. Each one receives a loan, but each member of the group cross-guarantees the loans of the other members. In other words, if José does not repay the loan, his friends have to cover for him. (Peer pressure turned positive.)

José puts the loan to good use. With the extra capital he is able to reduce his purchasing trips to once a week and keep his store open all day. After two years of growing his business and paying back his loans, he saves a thousand dollars, buys a plot of land in the favela, and is collecting cinder blocks for a house.[1]

How did this happen? Whom did God use to help José Ferreira? A taxi driver. A humanitarian organization. Fellow favela dwellers. They all worked together. Isn't this how God works?

This is how he worked in Jerusalem. The congregation is a microcosm of God's plan. No one can do everything, but everyone can do something. And when we do, statements such as these will be read more often: "The apostles testified powerfully to the resurrection of the Lord Jesus, and God's great blessing was upon them all. *There were no needy people among them*" (Acts 4:33–34 NLT).

Our only hope is to work together.

Some years back a reporter covering the conflict in Sarajevo saw a little girl shot by a sniper. The back of her head had been torn away by the bullet. The reporter threw down his pad and pencil and stopped being a reporter for a few minutes. He rushed to the man who was holding the child and helped them both into his car. As the reporter stepped on the accelerator, racing to the hospital, the man holding the bleeding child said, "Hurry, my friend. My child is still alive."

A moment or two later he pleaded, "Hurry, my friend. My child is still breathing."

A moment later, "Hurry, my friend. My child is still warm."

Finally, "Hurry. Oh my God, my child is getting cold."

By the time they arrived at the hospital, the little girl had died. As the two men were in the lavatory, washing the blood off their hands and their clothes, the man turned to the reporter and said, "This is a terrible task for me. I must go tell her father that his child is dead. He will be heartbroken."

The reporter was amazed. He looked at the grieving man and said, "I thought she was your child."

The man looked back and said, "No, but aren't they all our children?"[2]

Indeed. Those who suffer belong to all of us. And if all of us respond, there is hope.

Two are better than one,
*   because they have a good return for their work:*
If one falls down,
*   his friend can help him up.*
But pity the man who falls
*   and has no one to help him up!*

(Eccl. 4:9–10 NIV)

O Lord, I have been called to be part of a holy community. You did not call me in isolation but placed me in the body of Christ, along with every other believer in Jesus throughout the world in every age. Let us grow as a team, work as a team, worship as a team, weep, laugh, and live as a team. Grant me the wisdom and the strength to partner with you and with my brothers and sisters in Christ. For Jesus' sake and in his name I pray, amen.

CHAPTER 6

Open Your Door; Open Your Heart

They ate together in their homes,
happy to share their food with joyful hearts.

—ACTS 2:46 (NCV)

If a voice could be a season, hers was springtime. "Hello," she sang. "Thank you for calling." I needed a kind welcome. The sky was pouring buckets of rain. Lightning had caused blackouts, and storms were jamming the traffic. News reports were telling drivers to stay off the roads. But I had a flight to catch.

So I called the airlines. They would know if the flight was late or canceled. They would be the calm within the storm. And for a butterfly's blink of a moment, she was. "Hello, thank you for calling . . ."

But then it came. Before I could thank her in return, the voice continued, "For quality assurance this call may be monitored . . ."

Not again.

Ancient sailors feared falling off the edge of the earth. Our pioneering forefathers dreaded blinding blizzards. The first missionaries to Africa sliced trails into dense forests. But none of our ancestors faced what you and I face: the Bermuda Triangle called computerized telephone service.

"Press one," she said, "for domestic flights."

"Press two for international."

"Press three if you know your flight number and the name of your congressman."

"Press four if you are a frequent flier in the central time zone with no children."

"Press five if the nine digits of your Social Security number total more than sixty . . ."

It was all I could do to keep up! I finally pressed a number, and wouldn't you know it. I committed the equivalent of telephone hara-kiri. I was put on hold. For the foreseeable future I would be trapped in the underground cable cavern, doomed to spend hours listening to Kenny G and Barry Manilow.

Oh to have heard a human voice. To have spoken to a real person. To have received a human greeting. Is it just me, or is human contact going the way of the snow leopard? There was a time when every activity spurred a conversation. Service your car; greet the attendant. Deposit a check at the bank; chat with the teller about the weather. Buy a gift, and speak with the salesclerk. Not now. You can gas up with a credit card, make deposits online, and order a gift over the Internet. You can cycle through a day of business and never say *hello*.

Call us a fast society, an efficient society, but don't call us a personal society. Our society is set up for isolation. We wear earbuds when we exercise. We communicate via e-mail and text messages. We enter and exit our houses with gates and garage-door openers. Our mantra: "I leave you alone. You leave me alone."

Yet God wants his people to be an exception. Let everyone else go the way of computers and keyboards. God's children will be people of hospitality.

Long before the church had pulpits and baptisteries, she had kitchens and dinner tables. "The believers met together in the Temple every day. They ate together *in their homes*, happy to share their food with joyful hearts" (Acts 2:46 NCV). "Every day in the Temple and *in people's homes* they continued teaching the people and telling the Good News—that Jesus is the Christ" (Acts 5:42 NCV).

Even a casual reading of the New Testament unveils the house as the primary tool of the church. "To Philemon our beloved friend and fellow laborer . . . and to the church in your house" (Philem. vv. 1–2). "Greet Priscilla and Aquila . . . the church that is in their house" (Rom. 16:3, 5). "Greet the brethren who are in Laodicea, and Nymphas and the church that is in his house" (Col. 4:15).

It's no wonder that the elders were to be "given to hospitality" (1 Tim. 3:2 KJV). The primary gathering place of the church was the home.

Consider the genius of God's plan. The first generation of Christians was a tinderbox of contrasting cultures and backgrounds. At least fifteen different nationalities heard Peter's sermon on the Day of Pentecost. Jews stood next to Gentiles. Men worshipped with women. Slaves and masters alike sought after Christ. Can people of such varied backgrounds and cultures get along with each other?

We wonder the same thing today. Can Hispanics live in peace with Anglos? Can Democrats find common ground with Republicans? Can a Christian family carry on a civil friendship with the Muslim couple down the street? Can divergent people get along?

The early church did—without the aid of sanctuaries, church buildings, clergy, or seminaries. They did so through the clearest of messages (the Cross) and the simplest of tools (the home).

Not everyone can serve in a foreign land, lead a relief effort, or volunteer at the downtown soup kitchen. But who can't be hospitable?

Do you have a front door? A table? Chairs? Bread and meat for sandwiches? Congratulations! You just qualified to serve in the most ancient of ministries: hospitality. You can join the ranks of people such as . . .

Abraham. He fed, not just angels, but the Lord of angels (Gen. 18).

Rahab, the harlot. She received and protected the spies. Thanks to her kindness, her kindred survived, and her name is remembered (Josh. 6:22–23; Matt. 1:5).

Martha and Mary. They opened their home for Jesus. He, in turn, opened the grave of Lazarus for them (John 11:1–45; Luke 10:38–42).

Zacchaeus. He welcomed Jesus to his table. And Jesus left salvation as a thank-you gift (Luke 19:1–10).

And what about the greatest example of all—the "certain man" of Matthew 26:18? On the day before his death, Jesus told his followers, "Go into the city to a certain man and tell him, 'The Teacher says: "The chosen time is near. I will have the Passover with my followers at your house"'" (NCV).

How would you have liked to be the one who opened his home for Jesus? You can be. "Whatever you did for one of the least of these brothers of mine, you did for me" (Matt. 25:40 NIV). As you welcome strangers to your table, you are welcoming God himself.

Something holy happens around a dinner table that will never happen in a sanctuary. In a church auditorium you see the backs of heads. Around the table you see the expressions on faces. In the auditorium one person speaks; around the table everyone has a voice. Church services are on the clock. Around the table there is time to talk.

Hospitality opens the door to uncommon community.

It's no accident that *hospitality* and *hospital* come from the same Latin word, for they both lead to the same result: healing. When you open your door to someone, you are sending this message: "You matter to me and to God." You may think you are saying, "Come over for a visit." But what your guest hears is, "I'm worth the effort."

Do you know people who need this message? Singles who eat alone? Young couples who are far from home? Coworkers who've been transferred, teens who feel left out, and seniors who no longer drive? Some people pass an entire day with no meaningful contact with anyone else. Your hospitality can be their hospital. All you need are a few basic practices.

Issue a genuine invitation. Let your guests know you want them to come. Call them on the phone, or step over to their desks at work. Are they neighbors? Knock on their doors and say, "We'd love for you to join us at our dinner table tonight. Please come." People weather so many daily rejections. The doctor can't see them. The kids didn't call. The airplane is booked. But then you invite them over. *We have room for you!* Life altering.

Make a big deal of their arrival. Gather the entire family at the front door. Swing it open as you see them approach. If you have a driveway, meet them on it. If your apartment has a lobby, be waiting for them. This is a parade-worthy moment. One of God's children is coming to your house!

Address the needs of your guests. First-century hospitality included foot washing. Modern-day hospitality includes the sharing of food and drink. Time to talk and listen. No televisions blaring in the background. No invasive music. Make sure everyone has the opportunity to speak. Go around the table and share favorite moments of the day or memories of the week. Like the Good Shepherd, we prepare a table and restore the soul.

Send them out with a blessing. Make it clear you are glad your guests came. Offer a prayer for their safety and a word of encouragement for their travel.

The event need not be elaborate to be significant. Don't listen to the Martha Stewart voice, the voice that says everything must be perfect. The house must be perfect. The china must be perfect. Meal. Kids. Husband. Everything must be perfect. Scented guest towels, warm appetizers, after-dinner mints.

If we wait until everything is perfect, we'll never issue an invitation. Remember this: what is common to you is a banquet to someone else. You think your house is small, but to the lonely heart, it is a castle. You think the living room is a mess, but to the person whose life is a mess, your house is a sanctuary. You think the meal is simple, but to those who eat alone every night, pork and beans on paper plates tastes like filet mignon. What is small to you is huge to them.

Open your table.

Even more, open your circle. Be certain to invite not just the affluent and successful, "but when you give a banquet, invite the poor, the crippled, the lame, the blind, and you will be blessed" (Luke 14:13–14 NIV).

The Greek word for *hospitality* compounds two terms: *love* and *stranger*. The word literally means to love a stranger. All of us can welcome a guest we know and love. But can we welcome a stranger? Every morning in America more than 39 million people wake up in poverty.[1] In 2008, 17 million households had difficulty providing food for their families.[2] An estimated 1.1 million children lived in households experiencing hunger multiple times throughout the year.[3] And this is in America, the wealthiest nation in the history of the world.

When we provide food stamps, we stave off hunger. But when we invite the hungry to our tables, we address the deeper issues of value and self-worth. Who would have thought? God's secret weapons in the war on poverty include your kitchen table and mine.

A few months ago I was sitting at the red light of a busy intersection when I noticed a man walking toward my car. He stepped off the curb, bypassed several vehicles, and started waving at me. He carried a cardboard sign under his arm, a jammed pack on his back. His jeans were baggy, his beard was scraggly, and he was calling my name. "Max! Max! Remember me?"

I lowered my window. He smiled a toothless grin. "I still remember that burger you bought me." Then I remembered. Months, maybe a year earlier at this very intersection, I had taken him to a corner hamburger stand where we enjoyed a meal together. He was California bound on that day. "I'm passing through Texas again," he told me. The light changed, and cars began to honk. I pulled away, leaving him waving and shouting, "Thanks for the burger, Max."

I'd long since forgotten that meal. Not him. We never know what one meal will do.

In one of Jesus' resurrection appearances, he accompanies two disciples as they walk from Jerusalem to their village of Emmaus. The trail is a seven-mile journey, the better part of a day's walk for grown, healthy men. They converse the entire trip. Jesus gives them an overview of the Bible, beginning with the teachings of Moses right up to the events of their day. Still, they don't recognize him.

As they near their village, Jesus acts as if he is going to continue on his journey. We aren't told how he sent this message. Maybe he pulled out his pocket calendar and mumbled something about an evening appointment in the next town. We don't know how he left the impression, but he did.

The Emmaus-bound disciples had another idea. "But they urged him strongly, 'Stay with us, for it is nearly evening; the day is almost over'" (Luke 24:29 NIV).

It had been a long day. The two pilgrims had much on their minds. Certainly they had obligations and people in their lives. But their fellow traveler stirred a fire in their hearts. So they welcomed him in. Still not knowing that their guest was Jesus, they pulled out an extra chair, poured some water in the soup, and offered bread. Jesus blessed the bread, and when he did, "their eyes were opened and they recognized him" (v. 31 NIV).

We still encounter people on the road. And sometimes we sense a peculiar warmth, an affection. We detect an urge to open our doors to them. In these moments let's heed the inner voice. We never know whom we may be hosting for dinner.

Cheerfully share your home with those who need a meal or a place to stay. God has given each of you a gift from his great variety of spiritual gifts. Use them well to serve one another.

(1 Peter 4:9–10 NLT)

Heavenly Father, every breath is a gift from your hand. Even so, I confess that sometimes my own hand remains tightly closed when I encounter the needs of others. Please open both my hand and my heart that I might learn to open my door to others. As you help me open my heart and hand, O Lord, I ask that you also prompt me to open my life to those who need a taste of your love and bounty. In Jesus' name I pray, amen.

CHAPTER 7

See the Need;
Touch the Hurt

Peter, with John at his side, looked him straight in the eye . . . He grabbed him by the right hand and pulled him up.

—Acts 3:4, 7 (msg)

A gate called Beautiful. The man was anything but.

He couldn't walk but had to drag himself about on his knees. He passed his days among the contingent of real and pretend beggars who coveted the coins of the worshippers entering Solomon's court.

Peter and John were among them.

The needy man saw the apostles, lifted his voice, and begged for money. They had none to give, yet still they stopped. "Peter and John looked straight at him and said, 'Look at us!'" (Acts 3:4 NCV). They locked their eyes on his with such compassion that "he gave them his attention, expecting to receive something from them" (v. 5). Peter and John issued no embarrassed glance, irritated shrug, or cynical dismissal but an honest look.

It is hard to look suffering in the face. Wouldn't we rather turn away? Stare in a different direction? Fix our gaze on fairer objects? Human hurt is not easy on the eyes. The dusty cheeks of the Pakistani refugee. The wide-eyed stare of the Peruvian orphan. Or the salt-and-pepper tangle of a beard worn by the drifter Stanley and I met in Pennsylvania.

Stanley Shipp served as a father to my young faith. He was thirty years my senior and blessed with a hawkish nose, thin lips, a rim of white hair, and a heart as big as the Midwest. His business cards, which he gave to those who requested and those who didn't, read simply, "Stanley Shipp—Your Servant."

I spent my first postcollege year under his tutelage. One of our trips took us to a small church in rural Pennsylvania for a conference. He and I happened to be the only two people at the building when a drifter, wearing alcohol like a cheap perfume, knocked on the door. He recited his victim spiel. Overqualified for work. Unqualified for pension. Lost bus ticket. Bad back. His kids in Kansas didn't care. If bad breaks were rock and roll, this guy was Elvis. I crossed my arms, smirked, and gave Stanley a get-a-load-of-this-guy glance.

Stanley didn't return it. He devoted every optic nerve to the drifter. Stanley saw no one else but him. *How long*, I remember wondering, *since anyone looked this fellow square in the face?*

The meandering saga finally stopped, and Stanley led the man into the church kitchen and prepared him a plate of food and a sack of groceries. As we watched him leave, Stanley blinked back a tear and responded to my unsaid thoughts. "Max, I know he's probably lying. But what if just one part of his story was true?"

We both saw the man. I saw right through him. Stanley saw deep into him. There is something fundamentally good about taking time to see a person.

Simon the Pharisee once disdained Jesus' kindness toward a woman of questionable character. So Jesus tested him: "Do you *see* this woman?" (Luke 7:44).

Simon didn't. He saw a hussy, a streetwalker, a scamp. He didn't see the woman.

What do we see when we see . . .

- the figures beneath the overpass, encircling the fire in a fifty-five–gallon drum?
- the news clips of children in refugee camps?
- reports of 1.75 billion people who live on less than $1.25 a day?[1]

What do we see? "When He saw the multitudes, He was moved with compassion for them, because they were weary and scattered, like sheep having no shepherd" (Matt. 9:36).

This word *compassion* is one of the oddest in Scripture. The New Testament Greek lexicon says this word means "to be moved as to one's bowels . . . (for the bowels were thought to be the seat of love and pity)."[2] It shares a root system with *splanchnology*, the study of the visceral parts. Compassion, then, is a movement deep within—a kick in the gut.

Perhaps that is why we turn away. Who can bear such an emotion? Especially when we can do nothing about it. Why look suffering in the face if we can't make a difference?

Yet what if we could? What if our attention could reduce someone's pain? This is the promise of the encounter.

Then Peter said, "Silver and gold I do not have, but what I do have I give you: In the name of Jesus Christ of Nazareth, rise up and walk." And he took him by the right hand and lifted him up, and immediately his feet and ankle bones received strength. So he, leaping up, stood and walked and entered the temple with them—walking, leaping, and praising God. (Acts 3:6–8)

What if Peter had said, "Since I don't have any silver or gold, I'll keep my mouth shut"? But he didn't. He placed his mustard-seed-sized deed (a look and a touch) in the soil of God's love. And look what happened.

The thick, meaty hand of the fisherman reached for the frail, thin one of the beggar. Think Sistine Chapel and the high hand of God. One from above, the other from below. A holy helping hand. Peter lifted the man toward himself. The cripple swayed like a newborn calf finding its balance. It appeared as if the man would fall, but he didn't. He stood. And as he stood, he began to shout, and passersby began to stop. They stopped and watched the cripple skip.

Don't you think he did? Not at first, mind you. But after a careful step, then another few, don't you think he skipped a jig? Parading and waving the mat on which he had lived?

The crowd thickened around the trio. The apostles laughed as the beggar danced. Other beggars pressed toward the scene in their ragged coverings and tattered robes and cried out for their portion of a miracle.

"I want my healing! Touch me! Touch me!"

So Peter complied. He escorted them to the clinic of the Great Physician and invited them to take a seat. "His name, . . . faith in His name, has made this man strong . . . Repent therefore and be converted, that your sins may be blotted out, so that times of refreshing may come from the presence of the Lord" (vv. 16, 19).

Blotted out is a translation of a Greek term that means "to obliterate" or "erase completely." Faith in Christ, Peter explained, leads to a clean slate with God. What Jesus did for the legs of this cripple, he does for our souls. Brand-new!

An honest look led to a helping hand that led to a conversation about eternity. Works done in God's name long outlive our earthly lives.

Let's be the people who stop at the gate. Let's look at the hurting until we hurt with them. No hurrying past, turning away, or shifting of eyes. No pretending or glossing over. Let's look at the face until we see the person.

A couple in our congregation lives with the heartbreaking reality that their son is homeless. He ran away when he was seventeen, and with the exception of a few calls from prison and one visit, his parents have had no contact with him for twenty years. His mom allowed me to interview her at a leadership gathering. As we prepared for the discussion, I asked her why she was willing to disclose her story.

"I want to change the way people see the homeless. I want them to stop seeing problems and begin seeing mothers' sons."

In certain Zulu areas of South Africa, people greet each other with a phrase that means "I see you."[3] Change begins with a genuine look.

And continues with a helping hand. I'm writing this chapter by a dim light in an Ethiopian hotel only a few miles and hours removed from a modern-day version of this story.

Bzuneh Tulema lives in a two-room, dirt-floored, cinder-block house at the end of a dirt road in the dry hills of Adama. Maybe three hundred square feet. He's painted the walls a pastel blue and hung two pictures of Jesus, one of which bears the caption "Jesus the Goos [sic] Shepherd." During our visit the air is hot, the smell of cow manure is pungent, and I don't dare inhale too deeply for fear I'll swallow a fly.

Across from me, Bzuneh beams. He wears a Nike cap with a crooked bill, a red jacket (in spite of furnace-level heat), and a gap-toothed smile. No king was ever prouder of a castle than he is of his four walls. As the thirty-five-year-old relates his story, I understand.

Just two years ago he was the town drunk. He drank away his

first marriage and came within a prayer of doing the same with the second. He and his wife were so consumed with alcohol that they farmed out their kids to neighbors and resigned themselves to a drunken demise.

But then someone *saw* them. Like Peter and John saw the beggar, members of an area church took a good look at their situation. They began bringing the couple food and clothing. They invited them to attend worship services. Bzuneh was not interested. However, his wife, Bililie, was. She began to sober up and consider the story of Christ. The promise of a new life. The offer of a second chance. She believed.

Bzuneh was not so quick. He kept drinking until one night a year later he fell so hard he knocked a dent in his face that remains to this day. Friends found him in a gully and took him to the same church and shared the same Jesus with him. He hasn't touched a drop since.

The problem of poverty continued. The couple owned nothing more than their clothing and mud hut. Enter Meskerem Trango, a World Vision worker. He continued the looking-and-touching ministry. How could he help Bzuneh, a recovering alcoholic, get back on his feet? Jobs in the area were scarce. Besides, who would want to hire the village sot? A gift of cash was not the solution; the couple might drink it away.

Meskerem sat with Bzuneh and explored the options. He finally hit upon a solution. Cow manure. He arranged a loan through the World Vision microfinance department. Bzuneh acquired a cow, built a shed, and began trapping the cow droppings and turning them into methane and fertilizer. Bililie cooked with the gas, and he sold the fertilizer. Within a year Bzuneh had repaid the loan, bought four more cows, built his house, and reclaimed his kids.

"Now I have ten livestock, thirty goats, a TV set, a tape recorder, and a mobile phone. Even my wife has a mobile phone." He smiled. "And I dream of selling grain."

It all began with an honest look and a helping hand. Could this be God's strategy for human hurt? First, kind eyes meet desperate ones. Next, strong hands help weak ones. Then, the miracle of God. We do our small part, he does the big part, and life at the Beautiful Gate begins to be just that.

When Jesus landed and saw a large crowd, he had compassion
on them, because they were like sheep without a shepherd.

(Mark 6:34 NIV)

Gracious Lord, in the Bible you are called "the One who sees me," and I know that your eyes are always upon me to guide and protect and bless and correct. You have given me eyes too. Grant me the power to use them to truly *see*. Help me see those you put in my path—really see them, with all their hurts, their desires, their longings, their needs, their joys, and their challenges. As you open my eyes, prompt me to open wide my arms to offer whatever help and encouragement I have to give. In Jesus' name I pray, amen.

CHAPTER 8

Persecution:
Prepare for It; Resist It

The priests, the captain of the temple,
and the Sadducees came upon them.

—ACTS 4:1

On April 18, 2007, three Christians in Turkey were killed for their beliefs. Necati Aydin was one of them. He was a thirty-five-year-old pastor in the city of Malatya.

He nearly didn't go to his office that morning. He'd been traveling for ten days and his wife, Semse, wanted him to stay home and rest. She fed breakfast to their two children, Elisha and Esther, and took them to school. Upon returning, she walked softly so as not to awaken her husband. Even so, he stirred, squinted, opened his arms, and admitted his weariness. "I don't want to get up today."

But he did. There was much work to do. Only 0.2 percent of the mainly Muslim nation follows Jesus. Ironic. The land once knew the sandal prints of the apostle Paul and provided a stage for the first churches. But today? Turkish Christ worshippers number less than 153,000 in a nation of 76 million.[1] People such as Necati live to change that. He pulled his weary body out of bed and got ready for the day.

As Semse remembers and retells the events of that morning, she pauses between sentences. Her round cheeks flush with pink. Dark hair sweeps in a wave across her forehead. Until this point she's been able to contain the emotion. She described the attack, the cruelty, and the harshness of sudden widowhood without tears. But at this sentence, they press through. "My dear husband walked out the door at eleven. I was waiting for him to get on the elevator. There he smiled at me one last time, but I didn't know that was the last smile. That's what I'll always remember . . ."

She sighs and looks away as if seeing a face only she can see. Then back. "This is a painful thing for me because I miss his smile . . . because the sun doesn't rise when he doesn't smile . . ."

Semse looks down and permits a soft sob but only one. "It's a bitter cup, and we have to drink of it every day."

By the time Necati reached the office, his two colleagues had already received visitors: five young men who had expressed an interest in the Christian faith. But the inquisitors brought more than questions. They brought guns, bread knives, ropes, and towels.

The attackers brandished their weapons and told Necati to pray the Islamic prayer of conversion: "There is no God except Allah, and Muhammad is his prophet."

When Necati refused, the torture began. For an agonizing hour the assailants bound, interrogated, and cut the Christians. Finally, with the police pounding on the door, they sliced the throats of the victims. The last word heard from the office was the cry of an unswerving Christian: "Messiah! Messiah!"[2]

Such stories have a way of silencing us. This morning's traffic jam is no longer worth the mention. While I might see myself—for a microsecond—as a man of faith, I ponder the martyrs of Malatya and wonder, *Would I make the sacrifice? Would I cry out, "Messiah! Messiah!"? Would I give up my life?* Why, some days I don't want to give up my parking spot.

The Turkish pastors could have lived. With their simple confession of Allah, knives would have been lowered and lives spared. Semse would have her husband, and Elisha and Esther would have their father. Necati could have gone home to his family. He chose, instead, to speak up for Christ.

What would you have done?

The question is more than academic. Persecution comes. Three-fourths of Christians live in the third world, often in anti-Christian environments. More Chinese take part in Sunday worship than the entirety of western Europeans. Lebanon is 39 percent Christian; Sudan, 5 percent; Egypt, about 10 percent.³ Many of these saints worship at their own risk. You may be one of them. You may be the only Christian in your Iraqi university. You may be an Arab woman who offers prayers in silence or a Messianic Jew who lives in the heart of Jerusalem.

Or perhaps you indwell a society of religious freedom but a community of spiritual oppression. You may not face blades and terrorists but critics and accusers. Family members mock your beliefs. University professors belittle your convictions. Classmates snicker at your choices. Colleagues pressure you to compromise your integrity. Coworkers make it their mission to snag you in a weak moment. Knife to your neck? No. But pressure to abandon your convictions?

I'm thinking of Maria Dutton, my Portuguese teacher when I was a missionary in Brazil. She grew up in an aristocratic and influential family. When she became a Christian, her father disowned her. He didn't attend her wedding or see her at holidays. For several years he had nothing to do with her or her children.

Heidi is the only believer on the high school cheerleading squad. When the others go wild after games, she goes home. When they party on road trips, she goes to the hotel. She is the piñata for their ridicule.

Persecution happens. Peter and John can tell you. They healed the cripple one minute and faced harassment the next. "Now as they [Peter and John] spoke to the people, the priests, the captain of the temple, and the Sadducees came upon them, being greatly disturbed that they taught the people and preached in Jesus the resurrection from the dead" (Acts 4:1–2).

Thus far the early church had enjoyed smooth sailing. The Pentecost miracle harvested three thousand followers. The church gave birth to acts of kindness, compassion, and fellowship. Their good deeds authenticated their good news. The number of followers grew. The first three chapters of Acts are happy days. But then comes Acts 4. The church is barely out of the maternity ward, and in walk the town bullies: "the priests, the captain of the temple, and the Sadducees came upon them" (v. 1).

A brawny soldier presses through the crowd. He wears heavy ringlets of shoulder-length hair. His naked chest bulges, and his massive legs seem to be poured iron. A medallion of authority hangs on his chest, and he carries a whip in his hand. He can, by law, arrest anyone who transgresses the temple courts. He has come to enforce the law.

The priests follow him: Caiaphas and his father-in-law, Annas. They stand on either side of the temple captain and cross their arms and glare this implicit warning: "Don't forget what we did to your Messiah. Didn't the three spikes on the Roman cross make it clear?"

Annas, the high priest, arches an eyebrow in the direction of Peter. He has not forgotten what this apostle did to his servant a few weeks ago in the Garden of Gethsemane. When the servant and the soldiers came to arrest Jesus, Peter drew his sword and "struck the high priest's servant, and cut off his right ear" (John 18:10). Jesus healed the ear, but the high priest has not forgotten the incident. I'm envisioning Annas tugging his ear and menacing, "I have a score to settle with you, Peter."

Peter, meanwhile, may be wrestling with a few Thursday night memories of his own. Not just about his slashing sword, but also his dashing feet. He and the other followers scooted out of the garden like scalded puppies, leaving Jesus to face his foes all alone. Later that night Peter mustered up enough loyalty to appear at Jesus' trial. But when people recognized him, Peter wilted again. He denied his Savior, not once, but three times.

So far the score is Persecution–2, Peter–0. Peter has failed every test of persecution. But he won't fail this one.

The trio stands firm. If their legs tremble, it's because the beggar just learned to stand and the apostles are choosing not to run.

> Peter, filled with the Holy Spirit, said to them, "Rulers of the people and elders of Israel: If we this day are judged for a good deed done to a helpless man, by what means he has been made well, let it be known to you all, and to all the people of Israel, that by the name of Jesus Christ of Nazareth, whom you crucified, whom God raised from the dead, by Him this man stands here before you whole." (Acts 4:8–10)

No backdown in those words. I detect a touch of cynicism ("If we this day are judged for a good deed done to a helpless man . . .") and a large dose of declaration ("let it be known to you all, and to all the people of Israel, that by the name of Jesus Christ of Nazareth . . ."). Just the name Jesus would have sufficed, but Peter unapologetically replies, "Jesus Christ of Nazareth." And then he states clearly, potently, and firmly, "There is no other name under heaven given among men by which we must be saved" (v. 12).

Annas and Caiaphas snarl their lips. The temple captain squeezes his whip. The eyes of the Sadducees narrow into tiny slits. The power brokers of Jerusalem glare at Peter and John.

But they don't budge an inch. What has happened to them? The last time they saw these soldiers, Peter and John left them in their rearview mirror. But today they go chin to chin with the Supreme Court of Jerusalem. What's gotten into them?

Luke gives us the answer in verse 13: "Now when [the accusers] saw the boldness of Peter and John, and perceived that they were uneducated and untrained men, they marveled. And they realized that they had been with Jesus."

Peter and John had been with Jesus. The resurrected Jesus. In the Upper Room when he walked through the wall. Standing next to Thomas when the disciple touched the wounds. On the beach when Jesus cooked the fish. Sitting at Jesus' feet for forty days as he explained the ways of the kingdom.

They had lingered long and delightfully in the presence of the resurrected King. Awakening with him, walking with him. And because they had, silence was no longer an option. "We cannot but speak the things which we have seen and heard" (v. 20).

Could you use some high-octane boldness? If you want to outlive your life, you could. As long as you are stationary, no one will complain. Dogs don't bark at parked cars. But as soon as you accelerate—once you step out of drunkenness into sobriety, dishonesty into integrity, or lethargy into compassion—expect the yapping to begin. Expect to be criticized. Expect to be mocked. Expect to be persecuted.

So how can we prepare ourselves? Simple. Imitate the disciples. Linger long and often in the presence of Christ. Meditate on his grace. Ponder his love. Memorize his words. Gaze into his face. Talk to him. Courage comes as we live with Jesus.

Peter said it this way. "Don't give the opposition a second thought. Through thick and thin, keep your hearts at attention, in adoration before Christ, your Master. Be ready to speak up and tell anyone who asks why you're living the way you are, and always with the utmost courtesy" (1 Peter 3:14–15 MSG).

As we meditate on Christ's life, we find strength for our own. The example of Xu Yonghai comes to mind. A Christian in Communist China, he worked to see the legalization of house churches. The government responded by locking him in a Beijing prison for twenty-four months. His cell was eight-by-eight feet. There was no bathroom, only a pipe in a corner from which water flowed onto the concrete.

"My cell was the last stop for prisoners sentenced to die," he said. "At times there were as many as three other prisoners in the tiny, damp room, awaiting their date with the executioner."

Yonghai survived through prayer, meditation, and writing. On the walls of his cell, he wrote the major points for a book about God, using a bar of soap. Once he finished, he committed the thoughts to memory. Upon his release he turned his prison thoughts into a fifty-thousand-word book entitled *God the Creator*. Like Peter and John, Yonghai tarried in the presence of Jesus and found strength. Courage comes as we ponder the accomplishments of Christ.[4]

Would you be bold tomorrow? Then be with Jesus today. Be in his Word. Be with his people. Be in his presence. And when persecution comes (and it will), be strong. Who knows? People may realize that you, like the disciples, have been with Christ.

*You know how much persecution and suffering I have
endured. You know all about how I was persecuted in Antioch,
Iconium, and Lystra—but the Lord rescued me from all of
it. Yes, and everyone who wants to live a godly life in Christ
Jesus will suffer persecution.*

(2 Tim. 3:11–12 NLT)

Father, you warn us that persecution is coming. Not to alarm us but to prepare us for what's ahead—that we might endure and persevere. That these hard experiences would glorify you and benefit us. For that to happen, Lord, I need a reorientation of perspective and a change of focus. Help me see the world through your eyes by focusing on your son, remembering what he accomplished on the cross despite the persecution heaped on him. Whatever persecution I might suffer, Lord, let it bring you honor—and use it to help other followers of Jesus who will face their own persecution. In Christ's name I pray, amen.

CHAPTER 9

Do Good, Quietly

Ananias—his wife, Sapphira, conniving in this with him—sold a piece of land, secretly kept part of the price for himself, and then brought the rest to the apostles and made an offering of it.

—ACTS 5:1–2 (MSG)

The couple sat at the kitchen table and stared at the check for fifteen thousand dollars. The silence was a respite. The last half hour had been twelve rounds of verbal jabs and uppercuts. She blamed him for the idea. "You just had to give the money away."

He snapped back, "You didn't complain when everyone clapped for you at church, now did you?"

"Who would have thought that piece of dirt would bring this kind of price?"

Ananias hadn't expected to get fifteen thousand dollars. Ten thousand at best. Eight thousand at least. But fifteen thousand for an undeveloped acre off a one-lane road south of Jerusalem? He had inherited the property from his Uncle Ernie, who had left this note with the will: "Hang on to the land, Andy. You never know. If the road expands from one lane to four, you've got a nest egg."

So Ananias had taken the advice, locked the deed in a safe, and never thought about it until Sapphira, his wife, got wind of a generous deed done by Barnabas.

"He sold his beachfront condo and gave the money to the church."

"You're kidding. The condo in Jaffa?"

"That's what I heard."

"Whoa, that's prime real estate."

Ananias knew Barnabas from Rotary. Of course, everyone knew Barnabas. The guy had more friends than the temple had priests. Ananias couldn't help but notice the tone people used when discussing Barnabas's gift. Respect. Appreciation. *It would be nice to be thought of that way.*

So he mentioned the acre to Sapphira. "We're never going to build on it. I'm sure we can get eight thousand dollars. Let's give the money to the church."

"All of it?"

"Why not?"

They would have been better off just doing it, just keeping their mouths shut and giving the gift. They didn't need to tell a soul. But Ananias never excelled at mouth management.

During the next Sunday's worship service, the apostle Peter opened the floor for testimonials and prayer requests. Ananias popped up and took his place at the front.

"Sapphira and I've been blessed beyond words since coming here to the Jerusalem church. We want to say thank you. We are selling an acre, and we pledge to give every mite to the Widows' Fund."

The congregation, several thousand members strong, broke into applause. Ananias gestured for Sapphira to wave . . . she did. She stood and turned a full circle and blew a kiss toward Ananias. He returned the gesture and then saluted Peter. But Peter was not smiling. Ananias chose not to think much of it and stepped back to his seat. Later that night he called a real-estate agent and listed the property. He fell asleep with the thought of a foyer named after him.

Uncle Ernie's hunch about road expansion was spot-on. Two land developers wanted the property. Neither winced at the ten-thousand-dollar price tag. By the time the bidding was finished, the couple had a check for fifteen thousand.

So they sat at their kitchen table in silence. Sapphira stirred her coffee. Ananias stared at the check. It was Sapphira who first suggested the plan.

"What if we tell them we sold the property for just ten thousand dollars?"

"What?"

"Who has to know?"

Ananias thought for a moment. "Yeah, we'll just let everyone think we closed at ten thousand. That way we get credit for the gift and a little cash for something special."

She smiled. "Like a five-thousand-dollar down payment on a Jaffa condo?"

"No harm in that."

"No harm at all."

And so on the following Sunday, Ananias stood in front of the church again. He waved a check and announced, "We sold the property for ten thousand dollars!" and he placed the check in the offering basket. He basked in the applause and signaled for Sapphira to stand. She did.

They thought their cover-up was a success.

On Sunday afternoon the apostles called Ananias to a meeting.

"They surely want to thank us," he told Sapphira as he tightened his necktie. "Probably wondering if we'd be self-conscious at a recognition banquet."

"I'd be okay with one," she assured him.

He smiled and walked out the door, never thinking he wouldn't return.

According to Luke the meeting lasted only long enough for Peter to ask four questions and render a single verdict.

Question 1: "Ananias, why has Satan filled your heart to lie to the Holy Spirit and keep back part of the price of the land for yourself?" (Acts 5:3). So much for the cover-up. Luke's phrase for *keep back* means "misappropriate." The apostles sniffed out the couple's scheme for what it was: financial fraud.

Question 2: "While it remained, was it not your own?" (v. 4). No one forced the couple to sell the property. They acted of their own accord and free will.

Question 3: "After it was sold, was it not in your own control?" (v. 4). At any point the couple could have changed their minds or altered their contribution. The sin was not in keeping a portion of the proceeds but in pretending they gave it all. They wanted the appearance of sacrifice without the sacrifice.

Question 4: "Why have you conceived this thing in your heart?" (v. 4). This deceitful act was not an impulsive stumble but a calculated, premeditated swindle. Ananias had every intention of misleading the church. Did he not realize he was lying to God?

Peter made it clear with this verdict: "'You have not lied to men but to God.' Then Ananias, hearing these words, fell down and breathed his last" (vv. 4–5).

The body of Ananias was wrapped and buried before Sapphira had any clue what had happened. When she came to meet with Peter, she expected a word of appreciation. Peter gave her a chance to come clean.

"Tell me whether you sold the land for so much" (v. 8).

(Come on, Sapphira, tell the truth. You're in over your head. Just shoot straight, and you may live to tell about it.) She doesn't.

"Yes, for so much" (v. 8).

"How is it that you have agreed together to test the Spirit of the Lord? Look, the feet of those who have buried your husband are at the door, and they will carry you out" (v. 9).

As they carry Sapphira to join her husband in the cemetery, we shake our heads. Dare we wonder out loud what we're wondering inside? Ask the question we all think? Since no one else will ask it, I will.

Was that really necessary?

Ananias and Sapphira deserved punishment, for sure. They deserved a stiff sentence. But the death sentence? Does the punishment fit the crime? What they did was bad, but was it *that* bad?

Let's think about it. Exactly what did they do?

They used the church for self-promotion. They leveraged God's family for personal gain. They attempted to turn a congregation into a personal stage across which they could strut.

God has a strong word for such behavior: *hypocrisy*. When Jesus used it, people ducked for cover. He lambasted the Pharisees with this blowtorch:

> All their works they do to be seen by men . . . They love the best places at feasts, the best seats in the synagogues, greetings in the marketplaces, and to be called by men, "Rabbi, Rabbi." . . . But woe to you, scribes and Pharisees, hypocrites! For you shut up the kingdom of heaven against men . . . Woe to you, scribes and Pharisees, hypocrites! For you devour widows' houses, and for a pretense make long prayers . . . You cleanse the outside of the cup and dish, but

inside they are full of extortion and self-indulgence. (Matt. 23:5–7, 13–14, 25)

Jesus never spoke to anyone else with such intensity. But when he saw the religious hypocrite, he flipped on the spotlight and exposed every self-righteous mole and pimple. "They love to pray standing in the synagogues and on the corners of the streets, that they may be seen by men" (Matt. 6:5).

This is the working definition of *hypocrisy*: "to be seen by men." The Greek word for hypocrite, *hupokrites*, originally meant "actor." First-century actors wore masks. A hypocrite, then, is one who puts on a mask, a false face.

Jesus did not say, "Do not do good works." Nor did he instruct, "Do not let your works be seen." We must do good works, and some works, such as benevolence or teaching, must be seen in order to have an impact. So let's be clear. To do a good thing is a good thing. To do good to be seen is not. In fact, to do good to be seen is a serious offense. Here's why.

Hypocrisy turns people away from God. When God-hungry souls walk into a congregation of wannabe superstars, what happens? When God seekers see singers strut like Las Vegas entertainers . . . when they hear the preacher—a man of slick words, dress, and hair— play to the crowd and exclude God . . . when other attendees dress to be seen and make much to-do over their gifts and offerings . . . when people enter a church to see God yet can't see God because of the church, don't think for a second that God doesn't react. "Be especially careful when you are trying to be good so that you don't make a performance out of it. It might be good theater, but the God who made you won't be applauding" (Matt. 6:1 MSG).

Hypocrisy turns people against God. So God has a no-tolerance policy. Let the cold, lifeless bodies of the embezzling couple issue their intended warning. Let's take hypocrisy as seriously as God does. How can we?

1. *Expect no credit for good deeds.* None. If no one notices, you aren't disappointed. If someone does, you give the credit to God.

   Ask yourself this question: "If no one knew of the good I do, would I still do it?" If not, you're doing it to be seen by people.

2. *Give financial gifts in secret.* Money stirs the phony within us. We like to be seen earning it. And we like to be seen giving it. So "when you give to someone in need, don't let your left hand know what your right hand is doing" (Matt. 6:3 NLT).

3. *Don't fake spirituality.* When you go to church, don't select a seat just to be seen or sing just to be heard. If you raise your hands in worship, raise holy ones, not showy ones. When you talk, don't doctor your vocabulary with trendy religious terms. Nothing nauseates more than a fake "Praise the Lord" or a shallow "Hallelujah" or an insincere "Glory be to God."

Bottom line: don't make a theater production out of your faith. "Watch me! Watch me!" is a call used on the playground, not in God's kingdom. Silence the trumpets. Cancel the parade. Enough with the name-dropping. If accolades come, politely deflect them before you believe them. Slay the desire to be noticed. Stir the desire to serve God.

Heed the counsel of Christ: "First wash the inside of the cup and the dish, and then the outside will become clean, too" (Matt. 23:26 NLT). Focus on the inside, and the outside will take care of itself. Lay your motives before God daily, hourly. "Search me, O God, and know my heart; test me and know my anxious thoughts. Point out anything in me that offends you, and lead me along the path of everlasting life" (Ps. 139:23–24 NLT).

Do good things. Just don't do them to be noticed. You can be too good for your own good, you know.

But when you give to the needy, do not let your left hand know what your right hand is doing, so that your giving may be in secret. Then your Father, who sees what is done in secret, will reward you.

(Matt. 6:3–4 NIV)

Lord, you hate hypocrisy. It turns others away from you. Blunt my natural inclination to seek personal recognition for whatever good things you allow me to do. I don't want to be a phony, but neither do I want to be a glory hound. Fill me with your Spirit, and teach me to follow his example in gladly giving all glory to your Son. In Jesus' name I pray, amen.

CHAPTER 10

Stand Up
for the Have-Nots

The Greek-speaking widows were not given their share
when the food supplies were handed out each day.

—Acts 6:1 (cev)

Jim Wallis took some scissors to his Bible. He was a seminary student at Trinity Evangelical Divinity School when he and some classmates decided to eliminate a few verses. They performed surgery on all sixty-six books, beginning with Genesis and not stopping until Revelation. Each time a verse spoke to the topic of poverty, wealth, justice, or oppression, they cut it out. They wanted to see what a compassion-less Bible looked like. By the time they finished, nearly two thousand verses lay on the floor, and a book of tattered pages remained.[1]

Cut concern for the poor out of the Bible, and you cut the heart out of it. God makes the poor his priority. When the hungry pray, he listens. When orphans cry, he sees. And when the widows in Jerusalem were neglected, he commissioned his best and brightest disciples to help them.

Rapid church growth brought needy people, and among the needy people were widows. They had no source of income. When they buried their husbands, they buried their financial security. Government support? Company pension? The Widows Job Corp? Didn't exist. According to the culture of their day, the extended family provided support. But extended families disowned Christian relatives, leaving the widows of the church with only one place to turn: the church. The congregation responded with a daily distribution of food, clothing, and money.

That's when the trouble began.

But as the believers rapidly multiplied, there were rumblings of discontent. The Greek-speaking believers complained about the Hebrew-speaking believers, saying that their widows were being discriminated against in the daily distribution of food. (Acts 6:1 NLT)

The Greek-speaking widows were overlooked. Why? They were outsiders. Immigrants. These women didn't grow up in Judea or Galilee. They hailed from the distant lands of Greece, Rome, and Syria. If they spoke Aramaic at all, they did so with an accent.

Consequently, they were "neglected in the daily distribution" (NKJV). The driver of the Meals on Wheels truck skipped their houses. The manager of the food pantry permitted Hebrew women the first pick. The food bank director separated requests into two stacks: locals and immigrants.

How did the church respond? I'm picturing a called meeting of the apostles, a circle of bearded faces: Andrew, John, Peter, Thomas, and the others. They heard the concerns of the women and pondered their options. They could dismiss them entirely. They could ignore the needy, neglect the neglected. After all, the apostles were spiritual leaders. They fed souls, not stomachs. They dealt in matters of sin and salvation, not sandals and soup. Couldn't they dismiss the disparity as an unnecessary concern? They could, except for one problem. Their Master didn't.

Jesus, in his first message, declared his passion for the poor. Early in his ministry he returned to his hometown of Nazareth to deliver an inaugural address of sorts. He entered the same synagogue where he had worshipped as a young man and looked into the faces of the villagers. They were simple folk: stonecutters, carpenters, and craftsmen. They survived on minimal wages and lived beneath the shadow of Roman oppression. There wasn't much good news in Nazareth.

But this day was special. Jesus was in town. The hometown boy who had made the big time. They asked him to read Scripture, and he accepted. "And He was handed the book of the prophet Isaiah. And when He had opened the book, He found the place where it was written . . ." (Luke 4:17).

This is the only such moment in all the Gospels. Jesus *quoted* Scripture many times. But the Son of God, selecting and reading Scripture? This is it. On the singular occasion we know of, which verse did he choose? He shuffled the scroll toward the end of the text and read, "The Spirit of the LORD is upon Me, because He has anointed Me to preach the gospel to the poor; He has sent Me to heal the brokenhearted" (Luke 4:18, quoting Isaiah 61:1).

Jesus lifted his eyes from the parchment and quoted the rest of the words. The crowd, who cherished the words as much as he did, mouthed the lines along with him: "To proclaim liberty to the captives and recovery of sight to the blind, to set at liberty those who are oppressed; to proclaim the acceptable year of the LORD" (Luke 4:18–19).

Jesus had a target audience. The poor. The brokenhearted. Captives. The blind and oppressed.

His to-do list? Help for the body *and* soul, strength for the physical *and* the spiritual, therapy for the temporal *and* eternal. "This is my mission statement," Jesus declared. The Nazareth Manifesto.

Preach the gospel to the poor.

Heal the brokenhearted.

Proclaim liberty to the captives.

Proclaim recovery of sight to the blind.

Set at liberty those who are oppressed.

And proclaim the acceptable year of the Lord.

"Acceptable year of the LORD" describes, perhaps more than any other words, Jesus' radical commitment to the poor. They are reminiscent of the year of Jubilee, a twice-in-a-century celebration intended to press the restart button on the machinery of justice.[2] Beginning on the Day of Atonement, all the fields were allowed to rest. No farming permitted. The fallow land could recover from forty-nine years of planting and harvesting.

In addition, all the slaves were freed. Anyone who had been sold into slavery or who had sold himself into slavery to pay off debt was released. Bondage ended.

And as if the soil sabbatical and slave emancipation weren't enough, all property was returned to its original owners. In the agricultural society, land was capital. Families could lose their land through calamity, sickness, or even laziness. The Jubilee provision guaranteed that every family, at least twice a century, would have the opportunity to get back on its feet.

Consider the impact of this Jubilee decree. A drought destroys a farmer's crop and leaves the family impoverished. In order to survive, the farmer decides to sell his property and hire out as a day laborer. A sharp investor swoops into the region and buys the farm and also a neighbor's. Within short order the developer has a monopoly, and the farmer has nothing but a prayer.

But then comes the year of Jubilee, what one scholar described as a "regularly scheduled revolution."[3] God shakes the social Etch A Sketch, and everyone is given a clean slate. This injunction was intended to prevent a permanent underclass of poverty and slavery. People could still be rich, very rich, but they could not build their wealth on the backs of the very poor.

As far as we know, the people of Israel never practiced the year of Jubilee. Still, Jesus alluded to it in his inaugural address. What does this say about God's heart? At least this: he values a level playing field. In his society the Have-a-Lots and the Have-a-Littles are never to be so far apart that they can't see each other.

Can they see each other today?

Not very well. According to a United Nations Human Development Report, three-quarters of the world's income goes to 20 percent of the world's population.[4] Statistics can stagnate, so try this word picture.

Ten dairy farmers occupy the same valley. Among them, they own ten milk cows. But the cows aren't evenly distributed among the ten farmers—not one cow to one farmer. It's more like this: two of the farmers own eight cows, and the other eight farmers share two cows. Does that seem fair?

The two of us who own the eight cows might say, "I worked for my cows." Or "It's not my fault that we have more cows." Perhaps we should try this question: Why do a few of us have so much and most of us have so little?

I spent the better part of a morning pondering such a question on the Ethiopian farm of Dadhi. Dadhi is a sturdy but struggling husband and father. His dirt-floored mud hut would fit easily in my garage. His wife's handwoven baskets decorate his walls. Straw mats are rolled and stored against the sides, awaiting nightfall when all seven family members will sleep on them. Dadhi's five children smile quickly and hug tightly. They don't know how poor they are.

Dadhi does. He earns less than a dollar a day at a nearby farm. He'd work his own land, except a plague took the life of his ox. His only one. With no ox, he can't plow. With no plowed field, he can't sow a crop. If he can't sow a crop, he can't harvest one.

All he needs is an ox.

Dadhi is energetic and industrious. He has mastered a trade and been faithful to his wife. He's committed no crimes. Neighbors respect him. He seems every bit as intelligent as I am, likely more so. He and I share the same aspirations and dreams. I scribbled out a chart, listing our many mutual attributes.

Attributes	Dadhi	Max
Physically able	X	X
Willing to work	X	X
Trained to do a job	X	X
Loves family	X	X
Sober and drug free	X	X
Good reputation	X	You tell me

We have much in common. Then why the disparity? Why does it take Dadhi a year to earn what I can spend on a sport coat?

Part of the complex answer is this: he was born in the wrong place. He is, as Bono said, "an accident of latitude."[5] A latitude void of unemployment insurance, disability payments, college grants, Social

Security, and government supplements. A latitude largely vacant of libraries, vaccinations, clean water, and paved roads. I benefited from each of those. Dadhi has none of them.

In the game of life, many of us who cross home plate do so because we were born on third base. Others aren't even on a team.

You don't have to travel sixteen hours in a plane to find a Dadhi or two. They live in the convalescent home you pass on the way to work, gather at the unemployment office on the corner. They are the poor, the brokenhearted, the captives, and the blind.

Some people are poor because they are lazy. They need to get off their duffs. Others, however, are poor because parasites weaken their bodies, because they spend six hours a day collecting water, because rebel armies ravaged their farms, or because AIDS took their parents.

Couldn't such people use a bit of Jubilee?

Of course they could. So . . .

First, *let the church act on behalf of the poor*. The apostles did. "So the Twelve called a meeting of all the believers" (Acts 6:2 NLT). They assembled the entire church. The problem of inequity warranted a churchwide conversation. The leaders wanted every member to know that this church took poverty seriously. The ultimate solution to poverty is found in the compassion of God's people. Scripture endorses not forced communism but Spirit-led volunteerism among God's people.

Second, *let the brightest among us direct us*. "And so, brothers, select seven men who are well respected and are full of the Spirit and wisdom. We will give them this responsibility" (v. 3 NLT).

The first church meeting led to the first task force. The apostles unleashed their best people on their biggest problem. The challenge demands this. "Poverty," as Rich Stearns, president of World Vision in the United States, told me, "*is* rocket science." Simple solutions simply don't exist. Most of us don't know what to do about the avalanche of national debt, the withholding of lifesaving medicines, the corruption at the seaports, and the abduction of children. Most of us don't know what to do, but someone does!

Some people are pouring every ounce of God-given wisdom into the resolution of these problems. We need specialist organizations, such as World Vision, Compassion International, Living Water, and International Justice Mission. We need our brightest and best to continue the legacy of the Jerusalem task force of Acts 6.

And one more idea. *Get ticked off.* Riled up enough to respond. Righteous anger would do a world of good. Poverty is not the lack of charity but the lack of justice. Why *do* two of us have eight cows while the rest of us have two? Why do a billion people go to bed hungry every night?[6] Why do nearly thirty thousand children die every day, one every three seconds, from hunger and preventable diseases?[7] It's just not fair. Why not do something about it?

Again, no one can do everything, but everyone can do something. Some people can fast and pray about social sin. Others can study and speak out. What about you? Get out of your comfort zone for Christ's sake. Why not teach an inner-city Bible study? Use your vacation to build houses in hurricane-ravaged towns? Run for public office? Help a farmer get an ox?

Speaking of which, I received a note from Dadhi the other day. It included a photo of him and a new family member. A new three-hundred-pound, four-legged family member. Both of them were smiling. I'm thinking God was too.

Pure and genuine religion in the sight of God the Father means caring for orphans and widows in their distress and refusing to let the world corrupt you.

(James 1:27 NLT)

Dear Lord, you promised we would always have the poor among us. Help me to make sure that the reverse is also true: that I am always among the poor—helping, encouraging, and lending a hand wherever I can. Enable me to love the invisible God by serving the very visible poor in my corner of the world. Help me to be creative without being condescending, encouraging without being egotistic, and fearless without being foolish. May the poor bless you because of me, and may my efforts somehow reduce the number of the poor. In Jesus' name I pray, amen.

CHAPTER 11

Remember Who Holds You

Heaven is My throne, and earth is My footstool.
What house will you build for Me? says the LORD,
or what is the place of My rest? Has My hand not
made all these things?

—ACTS 7:49–50

When my nephew Lawson was three years old, he asked me to play some basketball. A towheaded spark plug of a boy, he delights in anything round and bouncy. When he spotted the basketball and goal in my driveway, he couldn't resist.

The ball, however, was as big as his midsection. The basket was three times his height. His best heaves fell way short. So I set out to help him. I lowered the goal from ten feet to eight feet. I led him closer to the target. I showed him how to "granny toss" the ball. Nothing helped. The ball never threatened the net. So I gave him a lift. With one hand on his back and my other beneath his little bottom, I lifted him higher and higher until he was eye level with the rim.

"Make a basket, Lawson!" I urged. And he did. He rolled the ball over the iron hoop, and down it dropped. *Swoosh!* And how did little Lawson respond? Still cradled in my hands, he punched both fists into the air and declared, "All by myself! All by myself!"

A bit of an overstatement, don't you think, little fellow? After all, who held you? Who steadied you? Who showed you the way? Aren't you forgetting somebody?

Stephen asked the same questions of the Jewish religious leaders.

He was one of the seven men tasked to care for the Gentile wid-ows. Luke describes him as "full of faith and power, [who] did great wonders and signs among the people" (Acts 6:8). His ministry, how-ever, provoked antagonism. A sect of jealous enemies falsely accused him of blasphemy. They marched him to the council of the Sanhedrin and demanded that he defend himself. Did he ever!

He caused a stir before he even opened his mouth. "Everyone in the high council stared at Stephen, because his face became as bright as an angel's" (Acts 6:15 NLT). Glowing cheeks. Light pouring through the pores of his face. Did his beard shimmer? Did heaven bathe him in a tunnel of brightness? I don't know how to imagine the scene. But I know how to interpret it. This was God speaking. The sermon emerges, not from Stephen's mind, but from God's heart. Every vowel, consonant, and clearing of the throat was his. This was no casual message.

Nor was it a lightweight message. Fifty-two verses that led the listeners from Abraham to Jesus. Two thousand years of Hebrew his-tory resulted in one indictment: "You're forgetting who holds you."

Stephen began with God's land grant.

Our glorious God appeared to our ancestor Abraham in Mesopotamia before he settled in Haran. God told him, "Leave your native land and your relatives, and come into the land that I will show you." So Abraham left the land of the Chaldeans and lived in Haran until his father died. Then God brought him here to the land where you now live. (Acts 7:2–4 NLT)

The only reason the Jews enjoyed a square inch of real estate was the kindness of God. He "appeared," "said," "promised," "spoke," "said," and "gave" (vv. 2, 3, 5, 6, 7, 8). Even then, Abraham's children almost squandered it away. They sold their brother into Egyptian slavery, divvied up the loot, and contrived a tale about an accidental death. The family lived with the lie for decades (vv. 9–15). Is this the way God's chosen people behave?

But God intervened. He "was with [Joseph]," "delivered," "gave him favor," "gave . . . wisdom," and "made [Joseph] governor" (vv. 9–10). When the people forgot God, God pursued the people.

Stephen continued with the story of Moses, "a beautiful child in God's eyes" (v. 20 NLT). Stephen recounted Moses' childhood among the Egyptians, his forty years of isolation, and his role as ruler and savior.

[Moses] led them out of Egypt, through the Red Sea, and through the wilderness for forty years . . .

Moses was with our ancestors, the assembly of God's people in the wilderness, when the angel spoke to him at Mount Sinai. And there Moses received life-giving words to pass on to us. (vv. 36, 38 NLT)

Once again God was the Great Initiator. He placed Moses in the household of Pharaoh and educated him in the Ivy League schools of Egypt. He trained him in the way of the wilderness and equipped him with the power to part the Red Sea. God gave food in the desert and the law on the mountain. And how did the people respond? They forgot him. They demanded return tickets on the first Greyhound back to Egypt. They actually made this request:

"Make us gods we can see and follow. This Moses who got us out here miles from nowhere—who knows what's happened to him!"

That was the time when they made a calf-idol, brought sacrifices to it, and congratulated each other on the wonderful religious program they had put together.

God wasn't at all pleased. (vv. 40–42 MSG)

Stephen's message echoed like the pounding of a kettledrum in the assembly hall. *Our ancestors forgot who brought us here. They forgot who carried us. They turned away from God, and now you've tried to put him in a box!*

Our fathers had the tabernacle of witness in the wilderness . . . until the days of David, who found favor before God and asked to find a dwelling for the God of Jacob. But Solomon built Him a house. (vv. 44–47)

Stephen wasn't showing disrespect to the tabernacle or the temple. Both were built in accordance with God's will. The mistake was not in their constructing the places of worship but in thinking the structures could contain God.

"However, the Most High does not dwell in temples made with hands, as the prophet says:

> *'Heaven is My throne,*
> *And earth is My footstool.*
> *What house will you build for Me? says the LORD,*
> *Or what is the place of My rest?*
> *Has My hand not made all these things?'* (vv. 48–50)

Translation? God cannot be localized. He has no address. No one has a monopoly on him. No temple can contain him.

These words didn't settle well with the Sanhedrin. The temple was the pride of the people: huge stones, glittering gold, massive archways, and, most of all, the Holy of Holies—the house of God. Jews kept this bumper sticker on their oxcarts: "Don't mess with the temple." Yet Stephen challenged their big heads with a huge point: *You've forgotten how big God is.*

So far, no good. You boast about a land you did not conquer, a law you did not follow, and a stone box that wouldn't encase God's pinkie finger. Your view of self? Too big. Your view of God? Too small. So small that you missed him when he came to town.

> Your ancestors killed anyone who dared talk about the coming of the Just One. And you've kept up the family tradition—traitors and murderers, all of you. You had God's Law handed to you by angels— gift-wrapped!—and you squandered it! (vv. 52–53 MSG)

Stephen might as well have told the Confederates that "Dixie" was a Yankee saloon song. The council stood in anger. They "gnashed at him with their teeth" (v. 54). They bared their fangs like angry jackals pouncing on fresh meat. "They . . . stopped their ears, and ran at him with one accord; and they cast him out of the city and stoned him" (vv. 57–58).

Frightening thing, this pride. It would rather kill the truth than consider it.

Doesn't it sneak up on us? We begin spiritual journeys as small people. The act of conversion is a humbling one. We confess sins, beg for mercy, bend our knees. We let someone lower us into the waters of baptism. We begin as self-effacing souls. Timid children who extend muddy hands to our sinless God. We relate to the thief on the cross, identify with David's forgiven adultery, and find hope in Peter's forgiven betrayal. We challenge Paul's claim to the chief-of-sinners title, wondering if anyone could need or treasure grace as much as we do.

We come to God humbly. No swagger, no boasts, no "all by myself" declarations. We flex no muscles and claim no achievements. We cup sullied hearts in hands and offer them to God as we would a crushed, scentless flower: "Can you bring life to this?"

And he does. *He* does. We don't. He works the miracle of salvation. He immerses us in mercy. He stitches together our shredded souls. He deposits his Spirit and implants heavenly gifts. Our big God blesses our small faith.

We understand the roles. He is the Milky Way galaxy. We are the sand flea. He is U2, and we are the neighborhood garage band, and that's okay. We need a big God because we've made a big mess of our lives.

Gradually our big God changes us. And, gratefully, we lust less, love more, lash out less, look heavenward more. We pay bills, pay attention to spouses, pay respect to parents. People notice the difference. They applaud us. Promote us. Admire us. Appoint us. We dare to outlive our lives. We—who came to Christ as sinful, soiled, and small—accomplish things. We build orphanages, lead companies, deliver the confused out of depression and the sick out of disease. Why, we even write books. We don't feel so small anymore. People talk to us as if we are something special.

"You have great influence."

"What strong faith you have."

"We need mighty saints like you."

Feels nice. Kudos become ladder rungs, and we begin to elevate ourselves. We shed our smallness, discard the Clark Kent glasses, and don a Superman swagger. We forget. We forget who brought us here.

We behave like a flea in the ear of a giraffe. The gangly animal breaks loose from the herd and charges across a wooden bridge. The worn-out bridge shivers and groans, barely able to support the weight. When they reach the other side, the flea puffs out its chest and declares, "Boy, did we shake that bridge."

We think we're shaking up the world when actually we're just along for the ride.

Take time to remember. "Look at what you were when God called you" (1 Cor. 1:26 NCV). Remember who held you in the beginning. Remember who holds you today.

Moses did. He served as the prince of Egypt and emancipator of the slaves, yet "Moses was . . . more humble than anyone else" (Num. 12:3 NIV). The apostle Paul knew to go low and not high. He was saved through a personal visit from Jesus, granted a vision of the heavens and the ability to raise the dead. But when he introduced himself, he simply stated, "I, Paul, am God's slave" (Titus 1:1 MSG). John the Baptist was a blood relative of Jesus and one of the most famous evangelists in history. But he is remembered in Scripture as the one who resolved: "He must increase, but I must decrease" (John 3:30).

And what about John Newton? This former slave trader served as a minister from 1764 until his death in 1807. He was a confidant of well-known leaders such as Hannah More and William Wilberforce. His hundreds of hymns fill churches with music. Yet on his deathbed the writer of the hymn "Amazing Grace" said these words to a young minister: "I'm going on before you, but you'll soon come after me.

When you arrive, our friendship will no doubt cause you to inquire for me. But I can tell you already where you'll most likely find me. I'll be sitting at the feet of the thief whom Jesus saved in His dying moments on the cross."[1]

John Newton never forgot who had lifted him up.

The greatest example of this humility is none other than Jesus Christ. Who had more reason to boast than he? Yet he never did. He walked on water but never strutted on the beach. He turned a basket into a buffet but never demanded applause. A liberator and a prophet came to visit him, but he never dropped names in his sermon. He could have. "Just the other day I was conferring with Moses and Elijah." But Jesus never thumped his chest. He refused even to take credit. "I can do nothing on my own" (John 5:30 NRSV). He was utterly reliant upon the Father and the Holy Spirit. "All by myself"? Jesus never spoke such words. If he didn't, how dare we?

We can rise too high but can never stoop too low. What gift are you giving that he did not first give? What truth are you teaching that he didn't first teach? You love. But who loved you first? You serve. But who served the most? What are you doing for God that he could not do alone?

How kind of him to use us. How wise of us to remember.

Stephen remembered. And since he remembered Jesus, Jesus remembered him. As Stephen's accusers reached for their rocks, he looked toward Christ. "Stephen, full of the Holy Spirit, gazed steadily into heaven and saw the glory of God, and he saw Jesus standing in the place of honor at God's right hand" (Acts 7:55 NLT).

Stephen stood on behalf of Christ, and in the end, Christ returned the favor.

What do you have that God hasn't given you?
And if everything you have is from God, why boast
as though it were not a gift?

(1 Cor. 4:7 NLT)

My Father, I desire that the attitude of John the Baptist might be my own—that Jesus would increase even as I decrease. Give me an ever-larger picture of you so I might see myself with ever-increasing clarity and revel each day in your amazing grace. Keep foolish pride far from me, and give me the sense to humble myself in healthy ways that bring strength and joy to everyone around me. Remind me constantly, Lord, that you hold my life and breath and eternal future in your loving hands and that every good thing I have comes from you. Never let me forget that although without you I can do nothing, in Christ I can do all things. The difference is you. In Jesus' name I pray, amen.

CHAPTER 12

Blast a Few Walls

"See, here is water. What hinders me
from being baptized?"
Then Philip said,
"If you believe with all your heart, you may."

—Acts 8:36–37

Fans rooted for the competition. Cheerleaders switched loyalties. The coach helped the opposition score points. Parents yelled for the competition.

What was this?

This was the brainchild of a big-hearted football coach in Grapevine, Texas. Kris Hogan skippers the successful program of Faith Christian High School. He has seventy players, eleven coaches, quality equipment, and parents who care, make banners, attend pep rallies, and wouldn't miss a game for their own funeral.

They took their 7–2 record into a contest with Gainesville State School. Gainesville's players, by contrast, wear seven-year-old shoulder pads and last decade's helmets and show up at each game wearing handcuffs. Their parents don't watch them play, but twelve uniformed officers do. That's because Gainesville is a maximum-security correctional facility. The school doesn't have a stadium, cheerleading squad, or half a hope of winning. Gainesville was 0–8 going into the Grapevine game. They'd scored two touchdowns all year.

The whole situation didn't seem fair. So Coach Hogan devised a plan. He asked the fans to step across the field and, for one night only, to cheer for the other side. More than two hundred volunteered.

They formed a forty-yard spirit line. They painted "Go Tornadoes!" on a banner that the Gainesville squad could burst through. They sat on the Gainesville side of the stadium. They even learned the names of Gainesville players so they could yell for individuals.

The prisoners had heard people scream their names but never like this. Gerald, a lineman who will serve three years, said, "People are a little afraid of us when we come to the games. You can see it in their eyes. They're lookin' at us like we're criminals. But these people, they were yellin' for us. By our names!"

After the game the teams gathered in the middle of the field to say a prayer. One of the incarcerated players asked to lead it. Coach Hogan agreed, not knowing what to expect. "Lord," the boy said, "I don't know how this happened, so I don't know how to say thank you, but I never would've known there was so many people in the world that cared about us."

Grapevine fans weren't finished. After the game they waited beside the Gainesville bus to give each player a good-bye gift—burger, fries, candy, soda, a Bible, an encouraging letter, and a round of applause. As their prison bus left the parking lot, the players pressed stunned faces against the windows and wondered what had just hit them.[1]

Here's what hit them: a squad of bigotry-demolition experts. Their assignment? Blast bias into dust. Their weapons? A fusillade of "You still matter" and "Someone still cares." Their mission? Break down barricades that separate God's children from each other.

Do any walls bisect your world? There you stand on one side. And on the other? The person you've learned to disregard, perhaps even disdain. The teen with the tats. The boss with the bucks. The immigrant with the hard-to-understand accent. The person on the opposite side of your political fence. The beggar who sits outside your church every week.

Or the Samaritans outside Jerusalem.

Talk about a wall, ancient and tall. "Jews," as John wrote in his gospel, "refuse to have anything to do with Samaritans" (John 4:9 NLT). The two cultures had hated each other for a thousand years. The feud involved claims of defection, intermarriage, and disloyalty to the temple. Samaritans were blacklisted. Their beds, utensils—even their spittle—were considered unclean.[2] No orthodox Jew would travel into the region. Most Jews would gladly double the length of their trips rather than go through Samaria.

Jesus, however, played by a different set of rules. He spent the better part of a day on the turf of a Samaritan woman, drinking water from her ladle, discussing her questions (John 4:1–26). He stepped across the cultural taboo as if it were a sleeping dog in the doorway. Jesus loves to break down walls.

That's why he sent Philip to Samaria.

Then Philip went down to the city of Samaria and preached Christ to them. And the multitudes with one accord heeded the things spoken by Philip, hearing and seeing the miracles which he did. For unclean spirits, crying with a loud voice, came out of many who were possessed; and many who were paralyzed and lame were healed . . .

When they believed Philip as he preached the things concerning the kingdom of God and the name of Jesus Christ, both men and women were baptized. (Acts 8:5–7, 12)

The city broke out into a revival. Peter and John heard about the response and traveled from Jerusalem to Samaria to confirm it. "When they had come down, [they] prayed for them that they might receive the Holy Spirit. For as yet He had fallen upon none of them. They had only been baptized in the name of the Lord Jesus. Then they laid hands on them, and they received the Holy Spirit" (vv. 15–17).

This is a curious turn of events. Why hadn't the Samaritans received the Holy Spirit? On the Day of Pentecost, Peter promised the gift of the Spirit to those who repented and were baptized. How then can we explain the baptism of the Samaritans, which, according to Luke, was not accompanied by the Spirit? Why delay the gift?

Simple. To celebrate the falling of a wall. The gospel, for the first time, was breaching an ancient bias. God marked the moment with a ticker-tape parade of sorts. He rolled out the welcome mat and sent his apostles to verify the revival and place hands on the Samaritans. Let any doubt be gone: God accepts all people.

But he wasn't finished. He sent Philip on a second cross-cultural mission.

Now an angel of the Lord spoke to Philip, saying, "Arise and go toward the south along the road which goes down from Jerusalem to Gaza." This is desert. So he arose and went. And behold, a man of Ethiopia, a eunuch of great authority under Candace the queen of the Ethiopians, who had charge of all her treasury, and had come to Jerusalem to worship, was returning. And sitting in his chariot, he was reading Isaiah the prophet. Then the Spirit said to Philip, "Go near and overtake this chariot." (vv. 26–29)

Walls separated Philip from the eunuch. The Ethiopian was dark skinned; Philip was light. The official hailed from distant Africa; Philip grew up nearby. The traveler was rich enough to travel. And who was Philip but a simple refugee, banished from Jerusalem? And don't overlook the delicate matter of differing testosterone levels. Philip, we later learn, was the father of four girls (Acts 21:9). The official was a eunuch. No wife or kids or plans for either. The lives of the two men could not have been more different.

But Philip didn't hesitate. He "preached Jesus to him. Now as they went down the road, they came to some water. And the eunuch said, 'See, here is water. What hinders me from being baptized?'" (Acts 8:35–36).

No small question. A black, influential, effeminate official from Africa turns to the white, simple, virile Christian from Jerusalem and asks, "Is there any reason I can't have what you have?"

What if Philip had said, "Now that you mention it, yes. Sorry. We don't take your type"?

But Philip, charter member of the bigotry-demolition team, blasted through the wall and invited, "'If you believe with all your heart, you may.' And he answered and said, 'I believe that Jesus Christ is the Son of God'" (v. 37).

Next thing you know, the eunuch is stepping out of the baptism waters, whistling "Jesus Loves Me," Philip is on to his next assignment, and the church has her first non-Jewish convert.

And we are a bit dizzy. What do we do with a chapter like this? Samaria. Peter and John arriving. Holy Spirit falling. Gaza. Ethiopian official. Philip. What do these events teach us? They teach us how God feels about the person on the other side of the wall.

He tore down the wall we used to keep each other at a distance . . .
Instead of continuing with two groups of people separated by cen-
turies of animosity and suspicion, he created a new kind of human
being, a fresh start for everybody.

Christ brought us together through his death on the cross. The
Cross got us to embrace, and that was the end of the hostility. (Eph.
2:14–16 MSG)

The cross of Christ creates a new people, a people unhindered
by skin color or family feud. A new citizenry, based not on common
ancestry or geography but on a common Savior.

My friend Buckner Fanning experienced this firsthand. He was a
marine in World War II, stationed in Nagasaki three weeks after the
dropping of the atomic bomb. Can you imagine a young American
soldier amid the rubble and wreckage of the demolished city? Radiation-
burned victims wandering the streets. Atomic fallout showering on the
city. Bodies burned to a casket black. Survivors shuffling through the
streets, searching for family, food, and hope. The conquering soldier,
feeling not victory but grief for the suffering around him.

Instead of anger and revenge, Buckner found an oasis of grace.
While patrolling the narrow streets, he came upon a sign that bore
an English phrase: Methodist Church. He noted the location and
resolved to return the next Sunday morning.

When he did, he entered a partially collapsed structure. Windows,
shattered. Walls, buckled. The young marine stepped through the
rubble, unsure how he would be received. Fifteen or so Japanese
were setting up chairs and removing debris. When the uniformed
American entered their midst, they stopped and turned.

He knew only one word in Japanese. He heard it. *Brother.* "They welcomed me as a friend," Buckner relates, the power of the moment still resonating more than sixty years after the events. They offered him a seat. He opened his Bible and, not understanding the sermon, sat and observed. During communion the worshippers brought him the elements. In that quiet moment the enmity of their nations and the hurt of the war was set aside as one Christian served another the body and blood of Christ.

Another wall came a-tumblin' down.

What walls are in your world?

Brian Overcast is knocking down walls in Morelia, Mexico. As director of the Noé Center (New Opportunities in Education), Brian and his team address the illegal immigration problem from a unique angle. Staff members told me recently, "Mexicans don't want to cross the border. If they could stay home, they would. But they can't because they can't get jobs. So we teach them English. With English skills they can get accepted into one of Mexico's low-cost universities and find a career at home. Others see illegal immigrants; we see opportunities."

Another wall down.

We can't outlive our lives if we can't get beyond our biases. Who are your Samaritans? Ethiopian eunuchs? Whom have you been taught to distrust and avoid?

It's time to remove a few bricks.

Welcome the day God takes you to your Samaria—not so distant in miles but different in styles, tastes, tongues, and traditions.

And if you meet an Ethiopian eunuch, so different yet so sincere, don't refuse that person. Don't let class, race, gender, politics, geography, or culture hinder God's work. For the end of the matter is this: when we cross the field and cheer for the other side, everyone wins.

Therefore, accept each other just as Christ has accepted you so that God will be given glory.

(Rom. 15:7 NLT)

Lord, in how many ways does my foolish heart make false distinctions among your people? Reveal them to me. How often do I judge someone as unworthy of you by the way I treat him or her? Rebuke me in your love. Where can I blast a wall or remove a barrier that keeps your children apart from one another? Give me some dynamite and the skill and courage to use it for your glory. What can I do in my sphere of influence to bring the love of Christ to someone who may feel ostracized or estranged from you? Lend me divine insight, and bless me with the resolve to be your hands and feet. May I be a bridge and not a wall. In Jesus' name I pray, amen.

CHAPTER 13

Don't Write Off Anyone

Brother Saul, the Lord Jesus, who appeared to you on the road as you came, has sent me that you may receive your sight and be filled with the Holy Spirit.

—Acts 9:17

Ananias hurries through the narrow Damascus streets.[1] His dense and bristling beard does not hide his serious face. Friends call as he passes, but he doesn't pause. He murmurs as he goes, "Saul? *Saul*? No way. Can't be true."

He wonders if he misheard the instructions. Wonders if he should turn around and inform his wife. Wonders if he should stop and tell someone where he is headed in case he never returns. But he doesn't. Friends would call him a fool. His wife would tell him not to go.

But he has to. He scampers through the courtyard of chickens, towering camels, and little donkeys. He steps past the shop of the tailor and doesn't respond to the greeting of the tanner. He keeps moving until he reaches the street called Straight. The inn has low arches and large rooms with mattresses. Nice by Damascus standards, the place of choice for any person of significance or power, and Saul is certainly both.

Ananias and the other Christians have been preparing for him. Some of the disciples have left the city. Others have gone into hiding. Saul's reputation as a Christian-killer preceded him. But the idea of Saul the Christ follower?

That was the message of the vision. Ananias replays it one more time.

"Arise and go to the street called Straight, and inquire at the house of Judas for one called Saul of Tarsus, for behold, he is praying. And in a vision he has seen a man named Ananias coming in and putting his hand on him, so that he might receive his sight" (Acts 9:11–12).

Ananias nearly choked on his matzo. *This isn't possible!* He reminded God of Saul's hard heart. "I have heard from many about this man, how much harm he has done to Your saints in Jerusalem" (v. 13). Saul a *Christian*? Sure, as soon as a turtle learns to two-step.

But God wasn't teasing. "Go, for he is a chosen vessel of Mine to bear My name before Gentiles, kings, and the children of Israel" (v. 15).

Ananias rehashes the words as he walks. The name Saul doesn't couple well with *chosen vessel*. Saul the thickhead—yes. Saul the critic—okay. But Saul the chosen vessel? Ananias shakes his head at the thought. By now he is halfway down Straight Street and seriously considering turning around and going home. He would have, except the two guards spot him.

"What brings you here?" they shout from the second story. They stand at attention. Their faces are wintry with unrest.

Ananias knows who they are—soldiers from the temple. Traveling companions of Saul.

"I've been sent to help the rabbi."

They lower their spears. "We hope you can. Something has happened to him. He doesn't eat or drink. Scarcely speaks."

Ananias can't turn back now. He ascends the stone stairs. The guards step aside, and Ananias steps into the doorway. He gasps at what he sees. A gaunt man sitting cross-legged on the floor, half shadowed by a shaft of sunlight. Hollow-cheeked and dry-lipped, he rocks back and forth, groaning a prayer.

"How long has he been like this?"

"Three days."

Saul's head sits large on his shoulders. He has a beaked nose and a bushy ridge for eyebrows. The food on the plate and the water in the cup sit untouched on the floor. His eyes stare out of their sockets in the direction of an open window. A crusty film covers them. Saul doesn't even wave the flies away from his face. Ananias hesitates. If this is a setup, he is history. If not, the moment is.

This encounter deserves something special: a drumroll, a stained-glass reenactment in a church window, some pages in a book called *You, on a Pew*? Before we read about Augustine and the child's voice or C. S. Lewis and the Inklings, we need to read about Saul, stubborn Saul, and the disciple who took a chance on him.

No one could fault Ananias's reluctance. Saul saw Christians as couriers of a plague. He stood near the high priest at Stephen's trial. He watched over the coats of stone-throwers at the execution. He nodded in approval at Stephen's final breath. And when the Sanhedrin needed a hit man to terrorize the church, Saul stepped forward. He became the Angel of Death. He descended on the Christians in a fury "uttering threats with every breath" (Acts 9:1 NLT). He "persecuted the church of God beyond measure and tried to destroy it" (Gal. 1:13).

Ananias knew what Saul had done to the church in Jerusalem. What he was about to learn, however, is what Jesus had done to Saul on the road to Damascus.

The trip was Saul's idea. The city had seen large numbers of conversions. When word of the revival reached Saul, he made his request: "Send me." So the fiery young Hebrew left Jerusalem on his

first missionary journey, hell-bent on stopping the church. The journey to Damascus was a long one, one hundred and fifty miles. Saul
likely rode horseback, careful to bypass the Gentile villages. This
was a holy journey.

It was also a hot journey. The lowland between Mount Hermon
and Damascus could melt silver. The sun struck like spears; the heat
made waves out of the horizon. Somewhere on this thirsty trail, Jesus
knocked Saul to the ground and asked him, "Saul, Saul, why are you
persecuting Me?" (Acts 9:4).

Saul jammed his fists into his eye sockets as if they were filled
with sand. He rolled onto his knees and lowered his head down to
the earth. "'Who are You, Lord?' Then the Lord said, 'I am Jesus,
whom you are persecuting'" (v. 5). When Saul lifted his head to look,
the living centers of his eyes had vanished. He was blind. He had the
vacant stare of a Roman statue.

His guards rushed to help. They led him to the Damascus inn and
walked with him up the stairwell.

By the time Ananias arrives, blind Saul has begun to see Jesus in
a different light.

Ananias enters and sits on the stone floor. He takes the hand of the
had-been terrorist and feels it tremble. He observes Saul's quivering
lips. Taking note of the sword and spear resting in the corner, Ananias
realizes Christ has already done the work. All that remains is for Ananias
to show Saul the next step. "Brother Saul . . ." (How sweet those words
must have sounded. Saul surely wept upon hearing them.)

> Brother Saul, the Lord Jesus, who appeared to you on the road as
> you came, has sent me that you may receive your sight and be filled
> with the Holy Spirit. (v. 17)

Tears rush like a tide against the crusts on Saul's eyes. The scaly covering loosens and falls away. He blinks and sees the face of his new friend.

Within the hour he's stepping out of the waters of baptism. Within a few days he's preaching in a synagogue. The first of a thousand sermons. Saul soon becomes Paul, and Paul preaches from the hills of Athens, pens letters from the bowels of prisons, and ultimately sires a genealogy of theologians, including Aquinas, Luther, and Calvin.

God used Paul to touch the world. But he first used Ananias to touch Paul. Has God given you a similar assignment? Has God given you a Saul?

A mother recently talked to me about her son. He's serving time in a maximum-security unit for robbery. Everyone else, even his father, has given up on the young man. But his mom has a different outlook. She really thinks her son's best years are ahead of him. "He's a good boy," she said firmly. "When he gets out of there, he's going to make something out of his life."

Another Saul, another Ananias.

I ran into a friend in a bookstore. He recently celebrated his fiftieth wedding anniversary. He teared up as he described the saint he married and the jerk his wife married. "I didn't believe in God. I didn't treat people with respect. Six weeks into the marriage, I came home one day to find her crying in the bathtub about the mistake she had made. But she never gave up on me."

Another Saul, another Ananias.

And you? Everyone else has written off your Saul. "He's too far gone." "She's too hard . . . too addicted . . . too old . . . too cold." No one gives your Saul a prayer. But you are beginning to realize that maybe God is at work behind the scenes. Maybe it's too soon to throw in the towel . . . You begin to believe.

Don't resist these thoughts.

Joseph didn't. His brothers sold him into Egyptian slavery. Yet he welcomed them into his palace.

David didn't. King Saul had a vendetta against David, but David had a soft spot for Saul. He called him "the LORD's anointed" (1 Sam. 24:10).

Hosea didn't. His wife, Gomer, was queen of the red-light district, but Hosea kept his front door open. And she came home.

Of course, no one believed in people more than Jesus did. He saw something in Peter worth developing, in the adulterous woman worth forgiving, and in John worth harnessing. He saw something in the thief on the cross, and what he saw was worth saving. And in the life of a wild-eyed, bloodthirsty extremist, he saw an apostle of grace. He believed in Saul. And he believed in Saul through Ananias.

"Brother Saul, the Lord Jesus, who appeared to you on the road as you came, has sent me that you may receive your sight and be filled with the Holy Spirit" (Acts 9:17).

Don't give up on your Saul. When others write him off, give him another chance. Stay strong. Call him brother. Call her sister. Tell your Saul about Jesus, and pray. And remember this: God never sends you where he hasn't already been. By the time you reach your Saul, who knows what you'll find.

My favorite Ananias-type story involves a couple of college roommates. The Ananias of the pair was a tolerant soul. He tolerated his friend's late-night drunkenness, midnight throw-ups, and all day sleep-ins. He didn't complain when his friend disappeared for the weekend or smoked cigarettes in the car. He could have requested a roommate who went to church more or cursed less or cared about something other than impressing girls.

But he hung with his personal Saul, seeming to think that something good could happen if the guy could pull his life together. So he kept cleaning up the mess, inviting his roommate to church, and covering his back.

I don't remember a bright light or a loud voice. I've never traveled a desert road to Damascus. But I distinctly remember Jesus knocking me off my perch and flipping on the light. It took four semesters, but Steve's example and Jesus' message finally got through.

So if this book lifts your spirit, you might thank God for my Ananias, Steve Green. Even more, you might listen to that voice in your heart and look on your map for a street called Straight.

I was shown mercy so that in me, the worst of sinners, Christ Jesus might display his unlimited patience as an example for those who would believe on him and receive eternal life.

(1 Tim. 1:16 NIV)

O Lord, *nobody* lies beyond the grasp of your grace. Who in my life do I see as hopeless? What man or woman who currently seems far from you do you want to bring into your family, in part through me? What Saul is out there to whom I could become an Ananias? Father, I pray that you would show your greatness and your power by using me in some way to introduce an "unlikely candidate" to your son. Help me triumph over my fears and obliterate my misconceptions as you work through me to bring someone else, through faith, into the circle of your love. In Jesus' name I pray, amen.

CHAPTER 14

Stable the High Horse

God has shown me that he doesn't think anyone
is unclean or unfit.

—Acts 10:28 (cev)

Molokai, a ruby on the pearl necklace of the Hawaiian Islands. Tourists travel to Molokai for its quiet charm, gentle breezes, and soft surf. But Father Damien came for a different reason. He came to help people die.

He came to Molokai because leprosy came here first. No one knows exactly how the disease reached Hawaii. The first documented case was dated around 1840. But while no one can trace the source of the disease, no one can deny its results. Disfigurement, decay, and panic.

The government responded with a civil version of Old Testament segregation. They deposited the diseased on a triangular thrust of land called Kalaupapa. Surrounded on three sides by water and on the fourth by the highest sea wall in the world, it was a natural prison.

Hard to get to. Harder still to get away from.

The lepers lived a discarded existence in shanties with minimal food. Ships would draw close to shore, and sailors would dump supplies into the water, hoping the crates would float toward land. Society sent the lepers a clear message: you aren't valuable anymore.

But Father Damien's message was different. He'd already served in the islands for a decade when, in 1873, at the age of thirty-three, he wrote his provincial and offered, "I want to sacrifice myself for the poor lepers."

He immersed himself in their world, dressing sores, hugging children, burying the dead. His choir members sang through rags, and congregants received communion with stumped hands. Because they mattered to God, they mattered to him. When he referred to his congregation, he didn't say "my brothers and sisters" but "we lepers." He became one of them. Literally.

Somewhere along the way, through a touch of kindness or in the sharing of a communion wafer, the disease passed from member to priest. Damien became a leper. And on April 15, 1889, four days shy of Good Friday, he died.[1]

We've learned to treat leprosy. We don't quarantine people anymore. We've done away with such settlements. But have we done away with the attitude? Do we still see some people as inferior?

We did on our elementary school playground. All the boys in Mrs. Amburgy's first-grade class bonded together to express our male superiority. We met daily at recess and, with arms interlocked, marched around the playground, shouting, "Boys are better than girls! Boys are better than girls!" Frankly, I didn't agree, but I enjoyed the fraternity. The girls, in response, formed their own club. They paraded around the school, announcing their disdain for boys. We were a happy campus.

People are prone to pecking orders. We love the high horse. The boy over the girl or girl over boy. The affluent over the destitute. The educated over the dropout. The old-timer over the newcomer. The Jew over the Gentile.

An impassable gulf yawned between Jews and Gentiles in the days of the early church. A Jew could not drink milk drawn by Gentiles or eat their food. Jews could not aid a Gentile mother in her hour of need. Jewish physicians could not attend to non-Jewish patients.[2]

No Jew would have anything to do with a Gentile. They were unclean.

Unless that Jew, of course, was Jesus. Suspicions of a new order began to surface because of his curious conversation with the Canaanite woman. Her daughter was dying, and her prayer was urgent. Yet her ancestry was Gentile. "I was sent only to help God's lost sheep—the people of Israel," Jesus told her. "That's true, Lord," she replied, "but even dogs are allowed to eat the scraps that fall beneath their masters' table" (Matt. 15:24, 27 NLT).

Jesus healed the woman's daughter and made his position clear. He was more concerned about bringing everyone in than shutting certain people out.

This was the tension Peter felt. His culture said, "Keep your distance from Gentiles." His Christ said, "Build bridges to Gentiles." And Peter had to make a choice. An encounter with Cornelius forced his decision.

Cornelius was an officer in the Roman army. Both Gentile and bad guy. (Think British redcoat in eighteenth-century Boston.) He ate the wrong food, hung with the wrong crowd, and swore allegiance to Caesar. He didn't quote the Torah or descend from Abraham. Toga on his body and ham in his freezer. No yarmulke on his head or beard on his face. Hardly deacon material. Uncircumcised, unkosher, unclean. Look at him.

Yet look at him again. Closely. He helped needy people and sympathized with Jewish ethics. He was kind and devout. "One who feared God with all his household, who gave alms generously to the people, and prayed to God always" (Acts 10:2). Cornelius was even on a first-name basis with an angel. The angel told him to get in touch with Peter, who was staying at a friend's house thirty miles away in the seaside town of Joppa. Cornelius sent three men to find him.

Peter, meanwhile, was doing his best to pray with a growling stomach. "He became very hungry and wanted to eat; but while they made ready, he fell into a trance and saw heaven opened and an object like a great sheet bound at the four corners, descending to him and let down to the earth. In it were all kinds of four-footed animals of the earth, wild beasts, creeping things, and birds of the air. And a voice came to him, 'Rise, Peter; kill and eat'" (vv. 10–13).

The sheet contained enough unkosher food to uncurl the payos of any Hasidic Jew. Peter absolutely and resolutely refused. "Not so, Lord! For I have never eaten anything common or unclean" (v. 14).

But God wasn't kidding about this. He three-peated the vision, leaving poor Peter in a quandary. Peter was pondering the pigs in the blanket when he heard a knock at the door. At the sound of the knock, he heard the call of God's Spirit in his heart. "Behold, three men are seeking you. Arise therefore, go down and go with them, doubting nothing; for I have sent them" (vv. 19–20).

"Doubting nothing" can also be translated "make no distinction" or "indulge in no prejudice" or "discard all partiality." This was a huge moment for Peter.

Much to his credit, Peter invited the messengers to spend the night and headed out the next morning to meet Cornelius. When Peter arrived, Cornelius fell at his feet. Peter insisted he stand up and then confessed how difficult this decision had been. "You know that we Jews are not allowed to have anything to do with other people. But God has shown me that he doesn't think anyone is unclean or unfit" (v. 28 CEV).

Peter told Cornelius about Jesus and the gospel, and before Peter could issue an invitation, the presence of the Spirit was among them, and they were replicating Pentecost—speaking in tongues and glorifying God. Peter offered to baptize Cornelius and his friends. They accepted. They offered him a bed. Peter accepted. By the end of the visit, he was making his own ham sandwiches.

And us? We are still pondering verse 28: "God has shown me that he doesn't think anyone is unclean or unfit."

Life is so much easier without this command. As long as we can call people common or unfit, we can plant them on Kalaupapa and go our separate ways. Labels relieve us of responsibility. Pigeonholing permits us to wash our hands and leave.

"Oh, I know John. He is an alcoholic." (Translation: "Why can't he control himself?")

"The new boss is a liberal Democrat." (Translation: "Can't he see how misguided he is?")

"Oh, I know her. She's divorced." (Translation: "She has a lot of baggage.")

Categorizing others creates distance and gives us a convenient exit strategy for avoiding involvement.

Jesus took an entirely different approach. He was all about including people, not excluding them. "The Word became flesh and blood, and moved into the neighborhood" (John 1:14 MSG). Jesus touched lepers and loved foreigners and spent so much time with partygoers that people called him a "lush, a friend of the riffraff" (Matt. 11:19 MSG).

Racism couldn't keep him from the Samaritan woman, demons

couldn't keep him from the demoniac. His Facebook page included the likes of Zacchaeus the Ponzi-meister, Matthew the IRS agent, and some floozy he met at Simon's house. Jesus spent thirty-three years walking in the mess of this world. "He had equal status with God but didn't think so much of himself that he had to cling to the advantages of that status no matter what. Not at all. When the time came, he set aside the privileges of deity and took on the status of a slave, became *human*!" (Phil. 2:6–7 MSG).

His example sends this message: no playground displays of superiority. "Don't call any person common or unfit."

My friend Roosevelt would agree. He is a leader in our congregation and one of the nicest guys in the history of humanity. He lives next door to a single mom who was cited by their homeowners' association for an unkempt lawn. A jungle of overgrown bushes and untrimmed trees obscured her house. The association warned her to get her yard cleaned up. The warning was followed by a police officer's visit. The officer gave her two weeks to do the work or appear in court. Her yard was a blight on the street, maybe even a health hazard.

Roosevelt, however, paid his neighbor, Terry, a visit. There is always a story behind the door, and he found a sad one. She had just weathered a rough divorce, was recovering from surgery, and was working a night shift at the hospital and extra hours to make ends meet. Her only son was stationed in Iraq. Terry was in survival mode: alone, sick, and exhausted. Lawn care? The least of her concerns.

So Roosevelt recruited several neighbors, and the families spent a Saturday morning getting things in order. They cut shrubs and branches and carted out a dozen bags of leaves. A few days later Terry sent this message to the board of the homeowners' association:

Dear Sirs,

I am hoping that you can make the neighborhood aware of what a great group of neighbors I have. These neighbors unselfishly toiled in my yard.

Their actions encouraged and reminded me that there are still some compassionate people residing here, people who care enough to reach out to strangers in their times of need to help lessen their burdens. These residents are to be commended, and I cannot adequately express how grateful I am for their hard work, positive attitude, and enthusiasm. This is all the more amazing considering my grandfather was a rabbi, and I have a mezuzah at my front door!

Roosevelt's response was a Christlike response. Rather than see people as problems, Christ saw them as opportunities.

May we consider a few more Cornelius moments?

You and your buddies enter the cafeteria, carrying your lunch trays. As you take your seat at the table, one of the guys elbows you and says, "Get a load of the new kid." You have no trouble spotting him. He's the only student wearing a turban. Your friend makes this wisecrack: "Still wearing his towel from the shower."

You might have made a joke yourself, except yesterday your pastor shared the story of Peter and Cornelius and read this verse: "God has shown me that he doesn't think anyone is unclean or unfit" (Acts 10:28 CEV).

Hmmm.

The guy in the next cubicle wears boots, chews tobacco, and drives a truck with a rifle rack. You wear loafers, eat health food, and drive a hybrid, except on Fridays when you pedal your bike to work. He makes racist jokes. Doesn't he notice that you are black? He has a Rebel flag as a screen saver. Your great-grandfather was a slave. You'd love to distance yourself from this redneck.

Yet this morning's Bible study included this challenge: "God has shown me that he doesn't think anyone is unclean or unfit" (v. 28 CEV).

Now what do you do?

One more. You are the superintendent of an orphanage. In dealing with the birth certificates, you come across a troubling word: *illegitimate*. As you research further, you learn that the word is a permanent label, never to be removed from the certificate.

This is what Edna Gladney discovered. And she couldn't bear the thought of it. If *legitimate* means to be legal, lawful, and valid, what does *illegitimate* mean? Can you imagine living with such a label?

Mrs. Gladney couldn't. It took her three years, but in 1936 she successfully lobbied the Texas legislature to remove the term from birth documents.[3]

God calls us to change the way we look at people. Not to see them as Gentiles or Jews, insiders or outsiders, liberals or conservatives. Not to label. To label is to libel. "We have stopped evaluating others from a human point of view" (2 Cor. 5:16 NLT).

Let's view people differently; let's view them as we do ourselves. Blemished, perhaps. Unfinished, for certain. Yet once rescued and restored, we may shed light, like the two stained-glass windows in my office.

My brother found them on a junkyard heap. Some church had discarded them. Dee, a handy carpenter, reclaimed them. He repainted the chipped wood, repaired the worn frame. He sealed some of the cracks in the colored glass. The windows aren't perfect. But if suspended where the sun can pass through, they cascade multicolored light into the room.

In our lifetimes you and I are going to come across some discarded people. Tossed out. Sometimes tossed out by a church. And we get to choose. Neglect or rescue? Label them or love them? We know Jesus' choice. Just look at what he did with us.

You [Jesus] are worthy to take the scroll
    and to open its seals,
because you were slain,
    and with your blood you purchased men for God
    from every tribe and language and people and nation.

(Rev. 5:9 NIV)

Father, you have used all types of people for your holy purposes:
prostitutes, murderers, persecutors, liars, thieves, swindlers, the
illiterate, the ignorant, the blind, the lame. Grant me the grace to
treat everyone I meet as someone for whom Jesus died and rose
again. Let there be no unwholesome or unholy distinctions in my eyes
and no unworthy favoritism in my actions. Rather, make me into a
vessel through whom Jesus shines. In Christ's name I pray, amen.

CHAPTER 15

Pray First; Pray Most

But while Peter was in prison,
the church prayed very earnestly for him.

—ACTS 12:5 (NLT)

King Herod suffered from a Hitler-level obsession with popularity. He murdered the apostle James to curry favor with the populace. The execution bumped his approval rating, so he jailed Peter and resolved to behead him on the anniversary of Jesus' death. (Would you like a little salt with that wound?)

He placed the apostle under the watchful eye of sixteen Navy Seal sorts and told them, with no tongue in cheek, "He escapes, you die." (Quality control, Herod style.) They bound Peter in chains and secured him three doors deep into the prison.

And what could the church do about it? The problem of an imprisoned Peter stood Goliath-tall over the humble community. They had no recourse: no clout, no political chips to cash. They had nothing but fear-drenched questions. "Who's next? First James, then Peter. Is Herod going to purge the church leadership?"

The church still faces her Goliaths. World hunger. Clergy scandal. Stingy Christians. Corrupt officials. Pea-brained and hard-hearted dictators. Peter in prison is just the first of a long list of challenges too big for the church.

So our Jerusalem ancestors left us a strategy. When the problem is bigger than we are—we pray! "But while Peter was in prison, the church prayed very earnestly for him" (Acts 12:5 NLT).

They didn't picket the prison, petition the government, protest the arrest, or prepare for Peter's funeral. They prayed. They prayed as if prayer was their only hope, for indeed it was. They prayed "very earnestly for him."

One of our Brazilian church leaders taught me something about earnest prayer. He met Christ during a yearlong stay in a drug-rehab center. His therapy included three one-hour sessions of prayer a day. Patients weren't required to pray, but they were required to attend the prayer meeting. Dozens of recovering drug addicts spent sixty uninterrupted minutes on their knees.

I expressed amazement and confessed that my prayers were short and formal. He invited (dared?) me to meet him for prayer. I did the next day. We knelt on the concrete floor of our small church auditorium and began to talk to God. Change that. I talked; he cried, wailed, begged, cajoled, and pleaded. He pounded his fists on the floor, shook a fist toward heaven, confessed, and reconfessed every sin. He recited every promise in the Bible as if God needed a reminder. He prayed like Moses.

When God determined to destroy the Israelites for their golden calf stunt, "Moses begged the LORD his God and said, 'LORD, don't let your anger destroy your people, whom you brought out of Egypt with your great power and strength. Don't let the people of Egypt say, "The LORD brought the Israelites out of Egypt for an evil purpose." . . . Remember the men who served you—Abraham, Isaac, and Israel. You promised with an oath to them'" (Ex. 32:11–13 NCV).

Moses on Mount Sinai is not calm and quiet, with folded hands and a serene expression. He's on his face one minute, in God's the next. He's on his knees, pointing his finger, lifting his hands. Shedding tears. Shredding his cloak. Wrestling like Jacob at Jabbok for the lives of his people.

And God heard him! "So the LORD changed his mind and did not destroy the people as he had said he might" (v. 14 NCV).

Our passionate prayers move the heart of God. "The effective, fervent prayer of a righteous man avails much" (James 5:16). Prayer does not change God's nature; who he is will never be altered. Prayer does, however, impact the flow of history. God has wired his world for power, but he calls on us to flip the switch.

And the Jerusalem church did just that.

The church prayed very earnestly for him.

The night before Peter was to be placed on trial, he was asleep, fastened with two chains between two soldiers. Others stood guard at the prison gate. Suddenly, there was a bright light in the cell, and an angel of the Lord stood before Peter. The angel struck him on the side to awaken him and said, "Quick! Get up!" And the chains fell off his wrists. Then the angel told him, "Get dressed and put on your sandals." And he did. "Now put on your coat and follow me," the angel ordered. (Acts 12:5–8 NLT)

The apostle, who once wondered how Christ could sleep in a storm, now snoozes through his own.

Let's give this scene the chuckle it deserves. An angel descends from heaven onto earth. Only God knows how many demons he battled en route. He navigates the Jerusalem streets until he reaches Herod's prison. He passes through three sets of iron doors and a squad of soldiers until he stands in front of Peter. Brightness explodes like a July sun in Death Valley. But Peter sleeps through the wake-up call. The old fisherman dreams of Galilean sea bass.

"Peter."

No response.

"Peter!"

Zzzzz.

"Peter!!!"

Do angels elbow or *wing* people? Either way, shackles clang on the floor. The angel has to remind groggy Peter how to re-robe. *First your sandals. Now your robe.* Doors swing open in succession. And somewhere on the avenue to Mary's house, Peter realizes he isn't dreaming. The angel points him in the right direction and departs, muttering something about bringing a trumpet next time.

Rightly stunned, Peter walks to Mary's house. She, at that very hour, is hosting a prayer meeting on his behalf. His friends pack the place and fill the house with earnest intercession.

Peter surely smiles as he hears their prayers. He knocks on the door. The servant answers and, instead of opening it, races back to the prayer circle and announces:

"Peter is standing at the door!"

"You're out of your mind!" they said. When she insisted, they decided, "It must be his angel." (vv. 14–15 NLT)

I confess a sense of relief at that reading. Even the early followers struggled to believe God would hear them. Even when the answer knocked on the door, they hesitated.

We still do. Most of us struggle with prayer. We forget to pray, and when we remember, we hurry through prayers with hollow words.

Our minds drift; our thoughts scatter like a covey of quail. Why is this? Prayer requires minimal effort. No location is prescribed. No particular clothing is required. No title or office is stipulated. Yet you'd think we were wrestling a greased pig.

Speaking of pigs, Satan seeks to interrupt our prayers. Our battle with prayer is not entirely our fault. The devil knows the stories; he witnessed the angel in Peter's cell and the revival in Jerusalem. He knows what happens when we pray. "Our weapons have power from God that can destroy the enemy's strong places" (2 Cor. 10:4 NCV).

Satan is not troubled when Max writes books or prepares sermons, but his knobby knees tremble when Max prays. Satan does not stutter or stumble when you walk through church doors or attend committee meetings. Demons aren't flustered when you read this book. But the walls of hell shake when one person with an honest heart and faithful confession says, "Oh, God, how great thou art."

Satan keeps you and me from prayer. He tries to position himself between us and God. But he scampers like a spooked dog when we move forward. So let's do.

> Humble yourselves before God. Resist the devil, and he will flee from you. Come close to God, and God will come close to you. (James 4:7–8 NLT)

> The LORD is close to everyone who prays to him,
> to all who truly pray to him. (Ps. 145:18 NCV)

When the children of Israel went to battle against the Amalekites, Moses selected the mountain of prayer over the valley of battle (Ex. 17:8–13). The Israelites won.

When Abraham learned about the impending destruction of Sodom and Gomorrah, he "remained standing before the LORD" rather than rush out to warn the cities (Gen. 18:22 NIV).

Advisers informed Nehemiah that Jerusalem was in ruins. He laid a foundation of prayer before he laid a foundation of stone (Neh. 1:4).

Paul's letters contain more requests for prayer than they do appeals for money, possessions, or comforts.

And Jesus. Our prayerful Jesus.

Awaking early to pray (Mark 1:35).

Dismissing people to pray (Matt. 14:23).

Ascending a mountain to pray (Luke 9:28).

Crafting a model prayer to teach us to pray (Matt. 6:9–13).

Cleansing the temple so others could pray (Matt. 21:12–13).

Stepping into a garden to pray (Luke 22:39–46).

Jesus immersed his words and work in prayer. Powerful things happen when we do the same.

Peggy Smith was eighty-four years old. Her sister, Christine, was eighty-two. The years had taken sight from the first and bent the body of the second. Neither could leave their house to attend church.

Yet their church needed them. They lived on the Isle of Lewis, off the coast of Scotland. A spiritual darkness had settled upon their village of Barvas. The congregation was losing people, and the youth were mocking the faith, speaking of conversion as a plague. In October 1949 the Presbytery of Free Church called upon their members to pray.

But what could two elderly, housebound sisters do? Quite a lot, they determined. They turned their cottage into an all-night house of prayer. From 10 p.m. to 4 a.m., two nights each week, they asked God to have mercy on their city. After several months Peggy told

Christine that God had spoken these words to her: "I will pour water upon him who is thirsty, and floods upon the dry ground."

She was so sure of the message, she urged her pastor to conduct a revival and invite well-known evangelist Duncan Campbell to speak. The pastor did, but Campbell reluctantly declined. Peggy received the news with confidence. "God hath said he is coming, and he will be here within a fortnight." God changed Campbell's calendar, and within two weeks the meeting began.

For five weeks Duncan Campbell preached in Barvas parish. Large crowds gathered in four services at 7 p.m., 10 p.m., midnight, and 3 a.m. The move of God upon the people was undeniable. Hundreds of people were converted. Drinking places closed for lack of patrons. Saloons emptied, and the church grew. The Isle of Lewis tasted the presence of God. All because two women prayed.[1]

So:

Let's pray, *first*. Traveling to help the hungry? Be sure to bathe your mission in prayer. Working to disentangle the knots of injustice? Pray. Weary of a world of racism and division? So is God. And he would love to talk to you about it.

Let's pray, *most*. Did God call us to preach without ceasing? Or teach without ceasing? Or have committee meetings without ceasing? Or sing without ceasing? No, but he did call us to "pray without ceasing" (1 Thess. 5:17).

Did Jesus declare: My house shall be called a house of study? Fellowship? Music? A house of exposition? A house of activities? No, but he did say, "My house will be called a house of prayer" (Mark 11:17 NIV).

No other spiritual activity is guaranteed such results. "When two of you get together on anything at all on earth and make a prayer of it, my Father in heaven goes into action" (Matt. 18:19 MSG). He is moved by the humble, prayerful heart.

In late 1964 Communist Simba rebels besieged the town of Bunia in Zaire. They arrested and executed many citizens. A pastor by the name of Zebedayo Idu was one of their victims. They sentenced him to death before a firing squad and placed him in jail for the night. The next morning he and a large number of prisoners were herded onto a truck and driven to a public place for execution. With no explanation the official told the prisoners to line up and number off—"one, two, one, two, one, two." The ones were placed in front of the firing squad. The twos were taken back to the prison. Pastor Zebedayo was among those who were spared.

Back in the jail cell, the prisoners could hear the sound of gunfire. The minister took advantage of the dramatic moment to share the story of Jesus and the hope of heaven. Eight of the prisoners gave their lives to God that day. About the time Pastor Idu finished sharing, an excited messenger came to the door with a release order. The pastor had been arrested by mistake and was free to leave.

He said good-bye to the prisoners and hurried to his home next to the chapel. There he discovered a crowd of believers urgently praying for his release. When they saw the answer to their prayers walk through the door, their prayer service became a praise service.[2]

The same God who heard the prayers from Jerusalem heard the prayers from Zaire. He is still listening. Are we still praying?

Devote yourselves to prayer with an alert mind and a thankful
heart. Pray for us, too, that God will give us many opportunities
to speak about his mysterious plan concerning Christ.

(Col. 4:2–3 NLT)

God of Abraham, Isaac, and Jacob, you created all that exists, and
you sustain all through your infinite wisdom and boundless power.
Yet you invite me to come to you in prayer, boldly and with the
expectation that you will hear and answer me. Teach me, Lord, to
take full advantage of this privilege, especially in regard to reaching
others with your love. Give me a heart for those who have yet to
experience the fullness of your grace, and prompt me to pray for
them and for their welfare, both in this world and in eternity. Lord,
bring me to the front lines of this battle. In Jesus' name I pray, amen.

CHAPTER 16

That's Jesus Playing That Fiddle

Whenever you did one of these things to someone
overlooked or ignored, that was me—you did it to me.

—Matthew 25:40 (msg)

At 7:51 a.m., January 12, 2007, a young musician took his position against a wall in a Washington, D.C., metro station. He wore jeans, a long-sleeved T-shirt, and a Washington Nationals baseball cap. He opened a violin case, removed his instrument, threw a few dollars and pocket change into the case as seed money, and began to play.

He played for the next forty-three minutes. He performed six classical pieces. During that time 1,097 people passed by. They tossed in money to the total of $32.17. Of the 1,097 people, seven—only seven—paused longer than sixty seconds. And of the seven, one—only one—recognized the violinist Joshua Bell.

Three days prior to this metro appearance staged by the *Washington Post*, Bell filled Boston's Symphony Hall, where just fairly good tickets went for $100 a seat. Two weeks after the experiment, he played for a standing-room-only audience in Bethesda, Maryland. Joshua Bell's talents can command $1,000 a minute. That day in the subway station, he barely earned enough to buy a cheap pair of shoes.

You can't fault the instrument. He played a Stradivarius built in the golden period of Stradivari's career. It's worth $3.5 million. You can't fault the music. Bell successfully played a piece from Johann

Sebastian Bach that Bell called "one of the greatest achievements of any man in history."

But scarcely anyone noticed. No one expected majesty in such a context. Shoe-shine stand to one side, kiosk to the other. People buying magazines, newspapers, chocolate bars, and lotto tickets. And who had time? This was a workday. This was the Washington workforce. Government workers mainly, on their way to budget meetings and management sessions. Who had time to notice beauty in the midst of busyness? Most did not.[1]

Most of us will someday realize that we didn't either. From the perspective of heaven, we'll look back on these days—these busy, cluttered days—and realize, *That was Jesus playing the violin. That was Jesus wearing the ragged clothes. That was Jesus in the orphanage . . . in the jail . . . in the cardboard shanty. The person needing my help was Jesus.*

There are many reasons to help people in need.

"Benevolence is good for the world."

"We all float on the same ocean. When the tide rises, it benefits everyone."

"To deliver someone from poverty is to unleash that person's potential as a researcher, educator, or doctor."

"As we reduce poverty and disease, we reduce war and atrocities. Healthy, happy people don't hurt each other."

Compassion has a dozen advocates.

But for the Christian, none is higher than this: when we love those in need, we are loving Jesus. It is a mystery beyond science, a truth beyond statistics. But it is a message that Jesus made crystal clear: when we love them, we love him.

This is the theme of his final sermon. The message he saved until last. He must want this point imprinted on our conscience. He depicted the final judgment scene. The last day, the great Day of Judgment. On that day Jesus will issue an irresistible command. All will come. From sunken ships and forgotten cemeteries, they will come. From royal tombs and grassy battlefields, they will come. From Abel, the first to die, to the person being buried at the moment Jesus calls, every human in history will be present.

All the angels will be present. The whole heavenly universe will witness the event. A staggering denouement. Jesus at some point will "separate them one from another, as a shepherd divides his sheep from the goats" (Matt. 25:32). Shepherds do this. They walk among the flock and, one by one, with the use of a staff direct goats in one direction and sheep in the other.

Graphic, this thought of the Good Shepherd stepping through the flock of humanity. You. Me. Our parents and kids. "Max, go this way." "Ronaldo, over there." "Maria, this side."

How can one envision this moment without the sudden appearance of this urgent question: What determines his choice? How does Jesus separate the people?

Jesus gives the answer. Those on the right, the sheep, will be those who fed him when he was hungry, brought him water when he was thirsty, gave him lodging when he was lonely, clothing when he was naked, and comfort when he was sick or imprisoned. The sign of the saved is their concern for those in need. Compassion does not save them—or us. Salvation is the work of Christ. Compassion is the consequence of salvation.

The sheep will react with a sincere question: When? When did we feed, visit, clothe, or comfort you (vv. 34–39)?

Jesus' answer will sound something like this. "Remember when you got off the subway? It was a wintry Washington morning. Commuters were bundled and busy and focused on their work. You were, too, mind you. But then you saw me. Yes, that was me! Standing between the coffee kiosk and the newsstand, that was me. I was wearing a baseball cap and a scarf and playing a fiddle. The mob rushed past as if I were a plastic plant. But you stopped. I knew you were busy. You looked at your watch twice. But still you stopped and remembered me. You stepped over to the coffee stand, bought me a cup, and brought it over. I want you to know I never forgot that."

Jesus will recount, one by one, all the acts of kindness. Every deed done to improve the lot of another person. Even the small ones. In fact, they all seem small. Giving water. Offering food. Sharing clothing. As Chrysostom pointed out, "We do not hear, 'I was sick and you *healed* me,' or 'I was in prison and you *liberated* me.'"[2] The works of mercy are simple deeds. And yet in these simple deeds, we serve Jesus. Astounding, this truth: we serve Christ by serving needy people.

The Jerusalem church understood this. How else can we explain their explosion across the world? We've only considered a handful of their stories. What began on Pentecost with the 120 disciples spilled into every corner of the world. Antioch. Corinth. Ephesus. Rome. The book of Acts, unlike other New Testament books, has no conclusion. That's because the work has not been finished.

Many years ago I heard a woman discuss this work. She visited a Catholic church in downtown Miami, Florida, in 1979. The small sanctuary overflowed with people. I was surprised. The event wasn't publicized. I happened to hear of the noon-hour presentation through a friend. I was living only a few blocks from the church. I showed up a few minutes early in hopes of a front-row seat. I should have arrived two hours early. People packed every pew and aisle. Some sat in windowsills. I found a spot against the back wall and waited. I don't know if the air-conditioning was broken or nonexistent, but the windows were open, and the south coast air was stuffy. The audience was chatty and restless. Yet when she entered the room, all stirring stopped.

No music. No long introduction. No fanfare from any public officials. No entourage. Just three, maybe four, younger versions of herself, the local priest, and her.

The father issued a brief word of welcome and told a joke about placing a milk crate behind the lectern so we could see his guest. He wasn't kidding. He positioned it, and she stepped up, and those blue eyes looked out at us. What a face. Vertical lines chiseled around her mouth. Her nose, larger than most women would prefer. Thin lips, as if drawn with a pencil, and a smile naked of pretense.

She wore her characteristic white Indian sari with a blue border that represented the Missionaries of Charity, the order she had founded in 1949. Her sixty-nine years had bent her already small frame. But there was nothing small about Mother Teresa's presence.

"Give me your unborn children," she offered. (Opening words or just the ones I remember most? I don't know.) "Don't abort them. If you cannot raise them, I will. They are precious to God."

Who would have ever pegged this slight Albanian woman as a change agent? Born in a cauldron of ethnic strife, the Balkans. Shy and introverted as a child. Of fragile health. One of three children. Daughter of a generous but unremarkable businessman. Yet somewhere along her journey, she became convinced that Jesus walked in the "distressing disguise of the poor," and she set out to love him by loving them. In 1989 she told a reporter that her Missionaries had picked up around fifty-four thousand people from the streets of Calcutta and that twenty-three thousand or so had died in their care.[3]

I wonder if God creates people like Mother Teresa so he can prove his point: "See, you can do something today that will outlive your life."

There are several billion reasons to consider his challenge. Some of them live in your neighborhood; others live in jungles you can't find and have names you can't pronounce. Some of them play in cardboard slums or sell sex on a busy street. Some of them walk three hours for water or wait all day for a shot of penicillin. Some of them brought their woes on themselves, and others inherited the mess from their parents.

None of us can help everyone. But all of us can help someone. And when we help them, we serve Jesus.

Who would want to miss a chance to do that?

Then the King will say to those on his right, "Come, you who are blessed by my Father, inherit the Kingdom prepared for you from the creation of the world. For I was hungry, and you fed me. I was thirsty, and you gave me a drink. I was a stranger, and you invited me into your home. I was naked, and you gave me clothing. I was sick, and you cared for me. I was in prison, and you visited me."

(Matt. 25:34–36 NLT)

O Lord, where did I see you yesterday . . . and didn't recognize you? Where will I encounter you today . . . and fail to identify you? O my Father, give me eyes to see, a heart to respond, and hands and feet to serve you wherever you encounter me! Transform me, Lord, by your Spirit into a servant of Christ, who delights to meet the needs of those around me. Make me a billboard of your grace, a living advertisement for the riches of your compassion. I long to hear you say to me one day, "Well done, good and faithful servant." And I pray that *today* I would be that faithful servant who does well at doing good. In Jesus' name I pray, amen.

Discussion and Action Guide

Prepared by David Drury

Max wants you to do more than read about the book of Acts. He wants you to live out the twenty-ninth chapter, writing the story of the church for your generation. *Outlive Your Life* urges you to reconsider your role in the world. The earliest Christians made ministry to the marginalized the center of their work. Jesus touched hurts, felt pain, and spoke grace. Following his example, the church exists to open doors, break walls, and restore relationships. If you want to go to the next level in being all Jesus Christ dreams for you and the church to be, the following pages will help you get started.

Use this guide to spark further reflection and inspire action related to the perspectives in *Outlive Your Life*. Each chapter in this guide includes Questions for Discussion that you can talk over in a group or consider on your own. You will also find Ideas for Action, which offer practical first steps in making a difference. Consider them. Then do them. Don't miss this opportunity to outlive your life.

CHAPTER 1: OUR ONCE-IN-HISTORY OPPORTUNITY

Questions for Discussion

1. How would you relate Ephesians 2:10 to the fable about Father Benjamin?

2. Describe someone you know who is outliving his or her life by meeting needs. In what ways do you want to be more like that person? What do the following passages tell you about outliving your life: Acts 13:22, 36; Isaiah 58:6–7; and Psalm 92:14?

3. Which needs break your heart the most? Share any statistics you have heard about that specific need, or return to pages 5–6 to review those offered. What words describe how you feel when you hear these numbers?

4. Max listed three questions that rocked his world. How might future generations be disappointed with the way we are responding to today's needs?

Ideas for Action

• Schedule time with someone you admire who's making a difference (perhaps the person you mentioned above). Ask these questions: Why did you choose to live this way? What motivates you? What did you have to learn? How did you begin?

- Intentionally expose yourself to a variety of needs. Create a list of ways to get out of your comfort zone and listen to people in need. Reorder your calendar to include projects that meet both local and global needs. Make sure your schedule includes something nearby (such as a neighborhood or community-action project) as well as something with international impact (perhaps a short-term missions trip).

CHAPTER 2: CALLING MR. POT ROAST

Questions for Discussion

1. Think about someone who did something ordinary for you, but it made an extraordinary difference. What small thing could you do that would have a big impact?

2. In what ways were the early disciples ordinary people? How would you have felt if you had been part of the 120 people who heard the words of Jesus just before he ascended (Acts 1:1–11)?

3. What lessons did you learn from the story of Nicholas Winton, who saved so many from the Holocaust? In what ways was he ordinary? What did you think of the fact that he didn't share the story with anyone until his wife discovered the scrapbook?

4. Review the idea of strengths and weaknesses presented in 2 Corinthians 12:9–10. Remember a time when you felt weak yet God gave you the strength to do something for him. Explain.

5. If Jesus told you to recruit eleven of your ordinary friends and relatives to change the world, whose names would you put on the list? How could your group make a difference right now?

Ideas for Action

- Engage in *routine* acts of kindness. Apply measurements of time to your service for others. Are you doing something daily, weekly, monthly, and yearly to show compassion and meet needs?

- Take part in *random* acts of kindness. Don't forget to work outside your routine as well. When God gives you an unplanned opportunity, react with compassion, and experience the joy of these divine appointments.

- Get involved in *radical* acts of kindness. Plan an intense, sacrificial, and strategic response to the needs of the world. Think big, get prepared, and enlist others to join you (start with the list of eleven people you created earlier).

CHAPTER 3: LET GOD UNSHELL YOU

Questions for Discussion

1. What habits, attitudes, possessions, and technologies create a clamshell of sorts to seal you off from the needs around you? How can you work around or remove these barriers?

2. Have you experienced what the chapter calls a "compassion attack"? Did you respond by ignoring the need or becoming distracted? Have you responded by trying to meet the need?

3. Describe a time when you saw God work in a sudden and unexpected way. To what extent are you open to the unexpected leadings of God? How could you prepare yourself for those times?

4. Respond to the following questions posed in the chapter:
   a. "With whom do you feel most fluent?" To what kinds of people or needs can you most easily relate?
   b. "For whom do you feel most compassion?" What kinds of needs touch your heart most deeply?

Ideas for Action

- Respond creatively to the needs around you. Here are a few ideas to get you started. Some people carry around fuel vouchers from the local gas station or free meal coupons from a nearby restaurant to give to people in need. Others have a special fund they are always prepared to use. Some individuals regularly give to a church benevolent fund and refer people to that church for aid. Plan *ahead* to respond with compassion (instead of waiting to see whether you feel like it in the moment).

- Consider focusing on one country with greater needs than your own in your prayers, giving, and relationships. Discover the true needs. Research what is working well. Find out what is not working. Pray intentionally. Eat their food. Celebrate their holidays. It might be possible to use your vacation time to go on a missions trip to that country.

- Research ministries or orphanages dedicated to that country's needs. Invest resources and build relationships. Make that country a second home in your heart. Over time you will be amazed by what God will do in and through you.

CHAPTER 4: DON'T FORGET THE BREAD

Questions for Discussion

1. Describe a time when you forgot something important.

2. What do the following verses encourage you to value most: Matthew 28:19; John 3:16; John 6:35; John 14:6; Romans 3:23; Romans 10:9; and Ephesians 2:8?

3. On a sheet of paper, make two lists side by side. In the first column, build a list of the most important things to God and the church. In the second column, make a list of the concerns that distract Christians from those most important things. At the bottom write down some practical ways to shift your focus from the second list to the first. Consider how focusing on the first list might also achieve the best concerns from the second list.

4. When has someone given you a second chance as the police officer gave Max? Think of a person who is looking for a second chance from you these days. How could you extend grace to that individual the next time you have the opportunity?

5. Grace gives not just "help for this life but hope for the next." Which do you find to be more important for people: tangible, *physical* needs or eternal, *spiritual* needs? In what situations do you need to meet a physical need first in order

to meet a deeper spiritual need? In what situations is the opposite true?

Ideas for Action

- When the people asked Peter, "Whatever could this mean?" it was an opportunity for him to speak about the most important things. If an acquaintance or friend said, "I've noticed something different about you—what is it?" it would be a great opportunity for you to do the same. Make a note of how you would answer that question.

- Pray for five friends, relatives, or acquaintances whom you think may be far from God. (If you simply do not know whether God is most important in a person's life, then he or she could be on this list.) For each of the five names, think of the next time you are likely to see that person. Make a personal commitment to pray daily for your "Five for God" list.

- Start a simple but intentional conversation with people about what is most important to you. Here are some ways to initiate the conversation:

  * "Would it be okay for me to tell you what's happened to me spiritually?"
  * "I want to make sure you know something about me—something I hope is true for you as well."
  * "Have I ever told you about the most important thing in my life?"

CHAPTER 5: TEAM UP

Questions for Discussion

1. When have you, as part of a group, faced a challenge so enormous that it caused the group to grow close? With what group of people are you facing a challenge right now, and how could you team up with them to face it?

2. What creative teamwork stories or opportunities have you heard that are like the microfinance story about José in Rio and Thomas in London? Do you know of anyone doing great work like this or responding to other areas of need? How do people get started making such innovative connections?

3. Consider traditional methods of helping people that also require teamwork. Have you ever been involved in these kinds of efforts? What was the impact on those in need? What did you learn from the experience?

4. "Those who suffer belong to all of us." How can you and the people closest to you lend a helping hand to those who suffer?

Ideas for Action

- "None of us can do what all of us can do." Become a part of something bigger than yourself. Tackle a very large project that you could not do alone by finding out what your church is already doing. It may not be what you would do on your own, but you will make a broader and deeper difference than if you worked alone.

- There are many ways to partner with a team that is already in tune with and actively responding to people's needs. Consider your own area of giftedness, and select a ministry that could use your talents to help others.
- Gather your neighbors to brainstorm needs in your area. Develop a plan of action that you can accomplish as a group.

Chapter 6: Open Your Door; Open Your Heart

Questions for Discussion

1. Do you know someone who is a great example of hospitality? What makes that person seem hospitable?

2. How are you currently using your home as a tool in helping others? How could you make your kitchen, your backyard, your living room, or even your dorm room into a place of intentional hospitality?

3. What keeps you from inviting others into your home? How could you remove those barriers? In what ways do you too often listen to the "Martha Stewart voice" and miss the point of hospitality?

4. Read each of the following passages about hospitality: Acts 16:15, 34; Acts 21:8; Acts 28:2, 7; Romans 12:13; 1 Timothy 5:10; Titus 1:8; Hebrews 13:2; 1 Peter 4:9–10; and 3 John 1:8. How should we view hospitality in light of these verses?

5. Name some people you would like to invite into your home soon. Set a time in the next two weeks to open your door to one or more of these people.

Ideas for Action

- Start a routine of hospitality in your life so it is always happening. Designate one meal a week as your "hospitality meal," and always plan to have people over. For example, you could invite friends every week to watch a ball game—an open invitation to enjoy your hospitality and your television. Or prepare a pot of soup every Saturday night. Set up a hospitality station on your front porch or in your driveway, and serve bowls of friendship to your neighbors.

- Intentionally include others at your special family events. Invite a single person over for Christmas Eve dinner. Have a family in need join you for Thanksgiving, or take the turkey and have the meal in *their* home. On Mother's Day celebrate some of the older women in church who never had children or whose children are far away. Keep an eye on individuals who sit alone or have yet to make friends in your church, and invite them over for a meal (even if you get take-out food on the way home).

CHAPTER 7: SEE THE NEED; TOUCH THE HURT

Questions for Discussion

1. "Human hurt is not easy on the eye." Tell of a time you encountered suffering that was painful to observe. Describe a time you were hurting and someone made you think he or she really *saw* you.

2. What does it communicate to people in need, especially those who are not beautiful, when you look directly at them, into their eyes?

3. Take note of each meaningful touch you find in the following miracles of Jesus: Matthew 9:20–22; Mark 1:40–45; Mark 7:32–35; Luke 8:51–55; Luke 13:11–13; John 9:1–7. Did Jesus need to touch people to heal them? Why do you think some form of touch was part of each healing?

4. Peter and John gave more than the money the crippled beggar asked for in Acts 3. What resources do you have—beyond money—that you could give to people in need?

5. For Peter and John the strategy of kind eyes meeting desperate ones and strong hands helping weak ones unleashed a miracle of God. How could you live out this strategy?

Ideas for Action

- Take time this week to look people in their eyes. When you talk to someone you know is needy, maintain eye contact with him or her much longer than you normally would. Reflect on how this helps you really *see* people's needs in a new way. It will have greater impact if you keep a journal or write a summary at the end of the week, describing how this experiment affected your perspective.

- This week, go out of your way to visit a person in need. When someone you know is in the hospital, visit that person to show you care. Go to a nursing home this week to extend a compassionate touch to others. Start by shaking people's hands or giving them an appropriate hug. Ask if you can pray for them, and lay a hand on their shoulders (you could even pray silently if you feel more comfortable doing so). As you head home, reflect on how meaningful the visit was. Also, consider how you feel after these visits, compared to how you felt on the way there.

CHAPTER 8: PERSECUTION: PREPARE FOR IT; RESIST IT

Questions for Discussion

1. How do you feel when you hear stories about heroic martyrs such as Necati or stories about horrible persecution around the world? In what ways does it put your own difficulties into perspective?

2. In societies with religious freedom, we may not experience persecution, but we may experience spiritual opposition from critics, accusers, family members, professors, classmates, coworkers, and others in our daily lives. As you read that list, does it remind you of a situation that led you to silence your beliefs?

3. How do you think Peter felt in John 18:15–18, 25–27? Have you ever failed to speak out in the face of pressure or persecution? On the other hand, when have you been like Peter before his accusers in Acts 4:5–13—ready to speak the truth boldly in the face of pressure or persecution?

4. What habits have you developed in order to spend time with Jesus so you can linger long and often in his presence? How could such habits help others realize you have been with him?

5. In what ways should spiritual disciplines develop boldness in a believer?

Ideas for Action

- Pray for the persecuted church. Become more knowledge-able about church freedom in a country you already have a connection with, and pray for the believers there to be strong in their faith. Stay current on the news about the church in that country.

- Rally your church to pray for persecuted believers by setting up a special prayer vigil or by participating in the Interna-tional Day of Prayer for the Persecuted Church. Consider buying a large world map for your home or church and hav-ing family or church members write prayers on Post-it notes and place them on the appropriate country.

Chapter 9: Do Good, Quietly

Questions for Discussion

1. The Acts 5 story of Ananias and Sapphira is an intense one. The consequences of their early church conspiracy were grave—literally. However, Max asks, "Was that really necessary?" What do you think?

2. How does the church regard such offenses today?

3. Have you seen examples of hypocrisy in the church that have adversely affected its reputation? What specific changes can Christians make to counter a general reputation for hypocrisy?

4. In Matthew 23, Jesus levels accusations against the Pharisees and scribes, or teachers of the law. List these seven indictments on a separate sheet of paper. How would you describe Jesus' tone in this passage? What common threads do you see in the list?

5. How will you live differently after reading Matthew 23, Acts 5, and this chapter of *Outlive Your Life*?

Ideas for Action

- "Expect no credit for good deeds." Think of someone you know who is in need. What tangible thing could you do for that person this week—in secret? Identify a person who has made a significant impact on your life. Send a letter thanking that individual for all he or she has done, but be sure the letter cannot be traced back to you.

- "Don't fake spirituality." Search the Scriptures to see what indicates false spirituality and what indicates authentic spirituality. Spend time in prayer, asking God to show you any area in which your spirituality is weak.

✸

CHAPTER 10: STAND UP FOR THE HAVE-NOTS

Questions for Discussion

1. The church in Jerusalem had overlooked Greek-speaking widows and sought to resolve the problem (Acts 6). What groups or individuals are overlooked in your community? Why are they forgotten or ignored?

2. Who is the target audience of your church? Describe the kind of person who is most likely to visit. If your church tried to become more like the people highlighted by Jesus in Luke 4:14–21, what adjustments would you have to make? What steps could you take to reach out to and worship with the poor, brokenhearted, captive, and blind?

3. Why do you think the people of Israel never practiced the revolutionary concept of Jubilee? Describe what Jubilee would look like in your area if this law went into effect immediately. What mini-Jubilees can you establish in your heart and habits even though this radical concept is not the law of the land?

4. Max mentioned several of the brightest and best organizations that are doing great work on poverty (World Vision, Compassion International, Living Water, and International Justice Mission). What organizations would you add, and why?

Ideas for Action

- This week find out more about what your church is already doing with the poor. Volunteer to get involved personally, to improve the work, or to fund it more intentionally.

- Rich Stearns told Max, "Poverty *is* rocket science." Consult the best thinkers on the more-complicated issues related to poverty. Learn about well-informed poverty solutions and strategies by visiting the Web sites of the excellent organizations mentioned in this chapter: www.wvi.org, www.compassion.com, www.water.cc, www.ijm.org.

- "Cut concern for the poor out of the Bible, and you cut the heart out of it." Take time this week to study just a few of the nearly two thousand scriptures on poverty, wealth, justice, and oppression. Start with the following verses:

    Exodus 23:6

    Leviticus 19:15; 23:22; 25:35, 39

    Deuteronomy 15:7–11; 24:10–15

    Psalm 35:10

    Proverbs 14:21; 22:22–23; 31:9

    Isaiah 10:1–3; 58:6–7

    Jeremiah 5:26–29

    Matthew 19:21

    Luke 12:32–33; 14:12–14

    Acts 4:33–35

    James 2:1–4

Chapter 11: Remember Who Holds You

Questions for Discussion

1. Which personal achievements make you feel most grateful? How much did God have to do with them? How could you thank God for his help and tell others about it?

2. In what seasons of life is it tempting to have a too-small view of God or a too-large view of yourself? What helpful habits could you develop to keep these two tendencies in check?

3. What instruction on pride and humility do you find in James 4:6–10? In what ways do you see humble people experiencing grace? When have you seen proud people opposed?

4. How does James 4:13–17 help you talk about the future with humility?

5. Humility and pride are opposites. However, wisdom may be a helpful path to cultivating humility and beating pride. How might a wise view of reality combat a too-high or too-low view of self?

Ideas for Action

- Do not miss what God is up to in your city. Use a journal to track moments when you see God moving. When did he show up in a way that you noticed? How did things go differently because someone was living as Christ would?

- The next time you receive praise, respond intentionally. Beware of dismissing it entirely by saying the accomplishment was nothing. Spread the praise around to others who helped you achieve it. Even better, praise others who helped, but then give God the glory for it all.

CHAPTER 12: BLAST A FEW WALLS

Questions for Discussion

1. Philip went to Samaria, and the grace of God blasted the walls between the Jews and Samaritans. Max asks you, "Do any walls bisect your world?" What divisions do you see dominating your culture? What unspoken rules of separation promote a subconscious prejudice? How long has this wall been there? What are the root causes? What keeps it going?

2. Describe yourself with the categories Max used to describe Philip (skin, hometown, economics, relationships, etc.). Now describe someone quite the opposite of you in these categories. Name someone you know who resembles the latter.

3. As Christians, how well do we live out Galatians 3:28–29 and erase the divisions between us? Where have we succeeded? Where have we failed?

4. How could you tell a person on the other side of a dividing wall that he or she matters to you? What could you do to show that person you care?

Ideas for Action

• Be honest with yourself about your prejudices. Spend some quiet time thinking about this. Make a list of groups of people you tend to prejudge or categorize. Pray over that piece of paper, asking God to change your heart. Then shred the list, embracing the freedom that comes with unbiased eyes.

- Grow in your cross-cultural awareness. Learn about the group that lives on the other side of a dividing social wall in your community or region. Eat where they eat, shop where they shop, and meet people. Listen to their stories. Find out what you have in common. Find out what differences are crucial, and be sensitive to them.

❀

CHAPTER 13: DON'T WRITE OFF ANYONE

Questions for Discussion

1. Name a very public or famous person whom nobody would expect to convert to Christianity. Why does it seem so unlikely that the person would become a Christian?

2. Share a story either about yourself or someone whom you know personally that made an unexpected radical conversion to God.

3. "Has God given you a Saul?" Is there someone in your life whom most people have given up on and dismissed? How could you be an Ananias for that person?

4. What does Scripture say about reaching out to those in need? How can you be more sensitive to the Father's promptings in this area?

5. How would you describe your conversion? Was it sudden or gradual? What are you doing to help others experience conversion?

Ideas for Action

- If you struggled to think of a potential Saul in your life, try to meet someone who could become that person. What kind of routine environment would help you become friends with people who are far from God—or even opposed to

God? Remember, God may be leading you to that place just as he led Ananias to Straight Street.

- Schedule time with a person who has converted to Christ and may need a mature Christian to disciple him or her. Start the process by simply asking that individual to retell his or her story, and then ask how you could help in the next leg of the journey.

CHAPTER 14: STABLE THE HIGH HORSE

Questions for Discussion

1. What was the social pecking order when you were growing up? How about today? Who is at the top, who is at the bottom, and where are you in the order?

2. In what situations do you hear offensive labeling? Have you found yourself inadvertently following suit? How can you be a leader of change in this environment?

3. Recall a time when you were in a situation similar to that of Peter in Acts 10. When have the customs or behaviors of another culture or race felt uncomfortable or even offensive to you? What would be your reaction if God called you to take up the habits and practices of others so you could reach out to them?

4. Why did Cornelius not look the part even though he was a Christ follower? What surface judgments do people use today to measure spirituality?

5. How could you make time for some marginalized Christians in your life?

Ideas for Action

- Make a new rule for the next two months: *No one sits alone.* When you enter any room, resist the urge to sit where you always sit and with the people you always join. First, scan the lunchroom or the boardroom, the stands or the sanctuary, the cafeteria or the theater, and find someone who is sitting alone. Then choose to sit with the marginalized. After two months you might consider making the rule permanent.

- Attend a worship service in a church with a predominantly different ethnicity or culture than your own. Adapt to that environment—do what they are doing as much as possible. Take note of what you admire about their worship and church life. Consider how it feels to be the odd man out. See what happens when, like Peter, you experience God within a different cultural setting.

CHAPTER 15: PRAY FIRST; PRAY MOST

Questions for Discussion

1. How would you describe the way Moses prayed to God in Exodus 32? In your own words, recount how Max describes the way his Brazilian church leader prayed. In what ways are your prayer times different from these descriptions? What could you do to become more fervent (passionate) in prayer?

2. What typical tactics does Satan use to keep you from prayer? How can you counter these with your own prayer strategies?

3. What is the role of prayer in the life of your church? How could you adjust your approach to prayer in your church to make it more meaningful?

4. Tell about a time when your prayer life seemed richer than it is now. What was different then?

5. What could you do to reenergize your prayer times? What postures could you take? What lists could you use? What prayer activities could you try? What scriptures could you use as prayers? Who could join you for prayer as an inspiration?

Ideas for Action

• Do a study this week on Jesus and prayer. Use the following verses from this chapter and other examples of Jesus praying or teaching about prayer to guide you:

Matthew 5:44; 6:6–13; 14:13, 23; 19:13; 21:12–13; 21:22; 24:20

Mark 1:35; 6:46; 9:28–29

Luke 6:12–16; 9:18–20; 18:1–8; 18:9–14; 22:39–46; 23:33–34

John 11:41; 17:1, 9, 20

- You may already pray before every meal and at the start of every day, but this week pray before you do these other things as well:

before you start your car

before you exercise

before you do the first thing you always do at work

before you turn on your computer

before you pick up the phone

before you go into a meeting

before you walk back into your home at the end of the day

before you turn on the television

before you open a book

before you go to sleep

before you _____

CHAPTER 16: THAT'S JESUS PLAYING THAT FIDDLE

Questions for Discussion

1. What various motivations move people to act compassionately?

2. For Christians, what is the key motivator to compassionate action?

3. On the Day of Judgment, how will Jesus separate the righteous from the unrighteous, according to Matthew 25:31–46? Why is this passage so hard to take at face value?

4. Which group was surprised at Jesus' choice in Matthew 25? Was it the sheep, the goats, or both? Why would they be surprised?

5. How are you trying to outlive your life now in ways you were not six months ago?

Ideas for Action

• Go back through this book in the next few days, and note the verses or quotes that most gripped your heart. On a separate sheet of paper or a few cards, write down these words and put them in a place that will keep the truths in front of you. Place them on your bathroom mirror, in your car, on your desk, in your purse, in your wallet, or on your door. Don't forget the message and mission you have taken from *Outlive Your Life*.

- Finalize your personal action plan with the goal of outliving your life. Determine how your gifts, passion, and opportunities best fit into God's plan to serve your neighborhood, community, and world. Overlay that template on your personal calendar to put your plan into action.

Notes

Chapter 1: Our Once-in-History Opportunity

1. UNICEF, *The State of the World's Children 2009: Maternal and Newborn Health*, www.unicef.org/sowc09/report/report.php.
2. Food and Agriculture Organization of the United Nations, *The State of Food Insecurity in the World: Economic Crises—Impacts and Lessons Learned*, 2, ftp://ftp.fao.org/docrep/fao/012/i0876e/i0876e.pdf.
3. UNICEF, *The State of the World's Children 2007: Women and Children; The Double Dividend of Gender Equality*, 5, www.unicef.org/sowc07/docs/sowc07.pdf.
4. That equals approximately 25,000 per day. Anup Shah, "Today, Over 25,000 Children Died Around the World," *Global Issues*, www.globalissues.org/article/715/today-over-25000-children-died-around-the-world.
5. Peter Greer and Phil Smith, *The Poor Will Be Glad: Joining the Revolution to Lift the World out of Poverty* (Grand Rapids: Zondervan, 2009), 26.
6. Ronald J. Sider, *Rich Christians in an Age of Hunger: Moving from Affluence to Generosity* (Nashville: Thomas Nelson, 2005), 10.
7. Ibid., 35.
8. UNICEF, *The State of the World's Children 2009*, 133.
9. The percentage of Christians in the United States is 76.8 percent, and the population of the United States in 2009 was approximately 307,212,000, according to the CIA, *The World Factbook*, 2009, https://www.cia.gov/library/publications/the-world-factbook/geos/us.html.
10. UNAIDS and World Health Organization, *AIDS Epidemic Update: November 2009*, 21, http://data.unaids.org/pub/Report/2009/JC1700_Epi_Update_2009_en.pdf.

Chapter 2: Calling Mr. Pot Roast

1. "Nicholas Winton, the Power of Good," Gelman Educational Foundation, www.powerofgood.net/story.php, and Patrick D. Odum, "Gratitude That Costs Us Something," *Heartlight*, www.heartlight.org/cgi/simplify .cgi?20090922_gratitude.html.

Chapter 3: Let God Unshell You

1. Hilary Le Cornu with Joseph Shulam, *A Commentary on the Jewish Roots of Acts* (Jerusalem: Netivyah Bible Instruction Ministry, 2003), 144.
2. Alfred Edersheim, *The Life and Times of Jesus the Messiah*, unabr. ed. (Peabody, MA: Hendrickson Publishers, Inc., 1993), 81–2.
3. M. Paul Lewis, ed., *Ethnologue: Languages of the World*, 16th ed. (Dallas: SIL International, 2009), www.ethnologue.com.
4. If you want to explore in detail your "you-niqueness" and how to discern it, see my book *Cure for the Common Life: Living in Your Sweet Spot* (Nashville: Thomas Nelson, 2005).
5. Telephone interview with Jo Anne Lyon, conducted by David Drury, June 23, 2009.

Chapter 5: Team Up

1. For an excellent summary of microfinance, see Peter Greer and Phil Smith, *The Poor Will Be Glad: Joining the Revolution to Lift the World out of Poverty* (Grand Rapids: Zondervan, 2009).
2. Sam Nunn, "Intellectual Honesty, Moral and Ethical Behavior; We Must Decide What Is Important" (speech, National Prayer Breakfast, Washington, D.C., February 1, 1996).

Chapter 6: Open Your Door; Open Your Heart

1. U.S. Bureau of the Census, *Poverty: 2007 and 2008; American Community Surveys*, 2, www.census.gov/prod/2009pubs/acsbr08-1.pdf.
2. Mark Nord, Margaret Andrews, Steven Carlson, *Household Food Security in the United States, 2008*, United States Department of Agriculture, iii, www.ers .usda.gov/Publications/ERR83/ERR83.pdf.
3. National and Community Service, "White House, USDA, National Service Agency, Launch Targeted Initiative to Address Hunger," www.nationalservice .gov/about/newsroom/releases_detail.asp?tbl_pr_id=1579.

Chapter 7: See the Need; Touch the Hurt

1. UNICEF, *The State of the World's Children 2009: Maternal and Newborn Health*, www.unicef.org/sowc09/report/report.php.

2. James Strong, *New Strong's Exhaustive Concordance* (Nashville: Thomas Nelson, 1996), s.v. "Compassion."

3. Bill Gates Sr. with Mary Ann Mackin, *Showing Up for Life: Thoughts on the Gifts of a Lifetime* (New York: Broadway Books, 2009), 155.

Chapter 8: Persecution: Prepare for It; Resist It

1. CIA, *The World Factbook*, 2009, https://www.cia.gov/library/publications/the-world-factbook/geos/tu.html.

2. *Malatya: The Story of the First Martyrs of the Modern Turkish Church*, www.malatyafilm.org.

3. CIA, *The World Factbook*, 2009, https://www.cia.gov/library/publications/the-world-factbook/index.html.

4. dc Talk and the Voice of the Martyrs, *Jesus Freaks: Stories of Those Who Stood for Jesus; The Ultimate Jesus Freaks* (Tulsa, OK: Albury Publishing, 1999), 208–9.

Chapter 10: Stand Up for the Have-Nots

1. Richard Stearns, *The Hole in Our Gospel* (Nashville: Thomas Nelson, 2008), 11.

2. *The Expositor's Bible Commentary with the New International Version of the Holy Bible* (Grand Rapids: Zondervan, 1990), 2:633–35.

3. Walter Bruggeman, "Isaiah and the Mission of the Church" (sermon, Mars Hill Bible Church, Grand Rapids, MI, July 13, 2008).

4. United Nations Development Programme, *Human Development Report 2007/2008: Fighting Climate Change; Human Solidarity in a Divided World*, 2007, 25, http://hdr.undp.org/en/media/HDR_20072008_EN_Complete.pdf.

5. "Closer to the Music," U2.com, July 30, 2003, www.u2.com/news/article/682.

6. United Nations World Food Programme, *WFP Facts Blast, December 2009*, http://home.wfp.org/stellent/groups/public/documents/communications/wfp187701.pdf.

7. Anup Shah, "Today, Over 25,000 Children Died Around the World," *Global Issues*, www.globalissues.org/article/715/today-over-25000-children-died-around-the-world.

Chapter 11: Remember Who Holds You

1. Mission Gate Ministry, "Gospel of Matthew, chapter 20," www.charityadvantage.com/MissionGateMinistry/images/Matt20.doc.

Chapter 12: Blast a Few Walls

1. Rick Reilly, "There Are Some Games in Which Cheering for the Other Side Feels Better Than Winning," *Life of Reilly*, http://sports.espn.go.com/espnmag/story?section=magazine&id=3789373.

2. Hilary Le Cornu with Joseph Shulam, *A Commentary on the Jewish Roots of Acts* (Jerusalem: Netivyah Bible Instruction Ministry, 2003), 403.

Chapter 13: Don't Write Off Anyone

1. Not to be confused with the Ananias of Acts 5.

Chapter 14: Stable the High Horse

1. Gavan Daws, *Holy Man: Father Damien of Molokai* (Honolulu: University of Hawaii Press, 1984).
2. Alfred Edersheim, *The Life and Times of Jesus the Messiah*, unabr. ed. (Peabody, MA: Hendrickson Publishers, Inc., 1993), 62–3.
3. Bob Ray Sanders, "*Blossom's in the Dust* Movie Fine, but the Woman Was Amazing," *Fort Worth Star Telegram*, November 17, 2002, www.angelfire.com/tx5/adoptee/sanders.html.

Chapter 15: Pray First; Pray Most

1. Oliver W. Price, "Needed: A Few Committed People to Pray for Revival," Bible Prayer Fellowship, www.praywithchrist.org/prayer/committed.php.
2. R. Kent Hughes, ed., *Acts: The Church Afire* (Wheaton, IL: Crossway Books, 1996), 169–70.

Chapter 16: That's Jesus Playing That Fiddle

1. Gene Weingarten, "Pearls before Breakfast," *Washington Post*, April 8, 2007, www.washingpost.com/wp-dyn/content/article/2007/04/04/AR2007040401721.html.
2. Frederick Dale Bruner, *The Churchbook: Matthew 13–28* (Dallas: Word Publishing, 1990), 918.
3. David Aikman, *Great Souls: Six Who Changed the Century* (Nashville: Word Publishing, 1998), 199–221, 224.

Tools for Your Church or Small Group

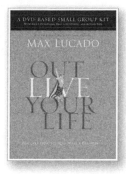

Outlive Your Life
DVD-Based Small Group Kit
978-1-4185-4394-5, $34.99

Join Max Lucado in this guided program to discover
how you can make a difference. You'll begin by following
the real-life stories of people like you who are making an
impact in their communities and around the world.
Then it's your turn. The Outlive Your Life program will
take you through daily readings, reflections, and action
plans so that each day you'll take another step toward
making your life count. Designed for individual study or
a small group experience, this study will make the
Outlive Your Life message a reality in your life.

   The kit includes a participant's guide, leader's guide,
and a CD-ROM with sermon notes and materials for
implementing a full church-wide campaign.

Outlive Your Life Participant's Guide
978-1-4185-4395-2, $9.99

This companion participant's guide for the *Outlive
Your Life DVD-Based Small Group Kit* is filled with
creative ideas and specific action plans that will guide
you through the daily process of taking action to
make your life count.

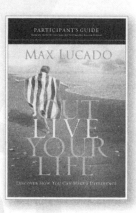

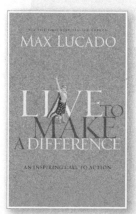

Live to Make a Difference
978-0-8499-4612-7, $2.99

Featuring key selections from *Outlive Your Life*, this
booklet embodies the spirit of making a difference in
the church as well as the local community, region, and
world. Perfect for giving away to your church
community, small group, or neighbors.

Inspiration for Every Day

You Changed My Life
978-1-4041-8783-2, $15.99

Sharing this inspiring message is the perfect way to thank teachers, pastors, and others who serve. This book also features a personal dedication page where givers are able to celebrate the persons who changed their lives.

DaySpring Outlive Your Life Product Collection

Outlive your life by encouraging others. Give a greeting card from Max's newly updated card line, a personal journal, or an inspirational Daybrightener® to someone special.

DaySpring.com

One Hand, Two Hands
978-1-4003-1649-6, $16.99

With whimsical words and delightful illustrations, Max shows how even the youngest children can serve others and how little helping hands bring joy to those being served, to the child and to our heavenly Father.

The Lucado Life Lessons Study Bible, NKJV
Hardcover
978-1-4185-4396-9, $49.99

Leathersoft black/gray,
978-1-4185-4398-3, $69.99

Leathersoft burgundy/gray,
978-1-4185-4399-0, $69.99

This beautifully designed Bible contains 1,000 practical application "Life Lessons," offering insights straight from Max Lucado's complete works, including *Outlive Your Life*.

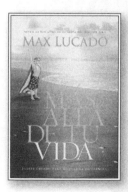

Outlive Your Life
Spanish Edition
978-1-6025-5404-7, $13.99

Outlive Your Life
Audiobook,
978-0-8499-4613-4, $24.99

Enjoy *Outlive Your Life* in Spanish or the unabridged audio.

For the Teens in Your Life

You Were Made to Make a Difference
978-1-4003-1600-7, $14.99

This adaptation of *Outlive Your Life* for teens
offers practical tips youth can take into their
communities to make a difference, plus
real-life stories about young people who
have done just that.

Made to Make a Difference
Youth Curriculum
978-1-5727-5266-5, $99.99

BluefishTV presents this
4-session DVD series that
follows the real-life stories of
teens who are trying to make
their lives count. With teaching
by Max Lucado and hosted by
Jenna Lucado Bishop, the study
explores how the church in Acts
left a legacy that students can
continue to build upon 2,000
years later.

BluefishTV.com

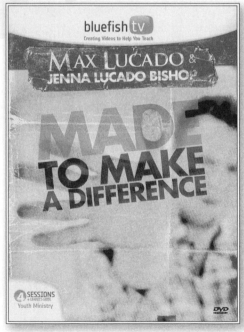

A Deeper Experience

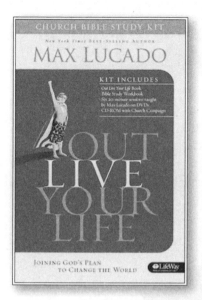

Church Bible Study
DVD Kit · 005189411
$49.95

Member Book · 005271299
$11.95

DVD Kit includes a Member Book
with facilitator notes, listening guide,
and daily devotionals; hardcover copy of
Outlive Your Life; a DVD with six videos
of Max; and a CD-ROM with leader
helps, preaching aids, and church-wide
campaign implementation plans.

Outlive Your Life CD
Songs Inspiring You to Make a Difference
$14.98

Music to inspire you to make a
difference, all on one CD,
featuring music from Travis
Cottrell, Lenny LeBlanc, Robin
Mark, Ali Rogers, and more.

Outlive Your Life DVD
Outlive Your Live Worship Elements
$14.98

Bring the *Outlive Your Life*
experience to your church with all
the multimedia elements on one
DVD. The Worship Elements
DVD features video motion, still
background templates, video
teaching moments with Max
Lucado, and more.

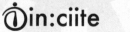